Neither East Nor West

FREEDOM PRESS CENTENARY SERIES
Supplement to
Volume 3. FROM WORLD WAR TO COLD WAR 1939-1950

FREEDOM PRESS publish *Freedom* (monthly) and *The Raven* (quarterly) as well as books (more than thirty titles in print). FREEDOM PRESS BOOKSHOP carries the most comprehensive stock of anarchist literature including titles from North America. Please send for our current list.
FREEDOM PRESS
in Angel Alley
84b Whitechapel High Street
London E1 7QX

FREEDOM PRESS CENTENARY VOLUMES

To mark the Centenary in 1986 of FREEDOM PRESS and of our journal *Freedom*, a special 88-page issue of *Freedom* was published with the title

FREEDOM / A HUNDRED YEARS / October 1886 to October 1986

In addition a series of six volumes, with supplements in some cases, will be published.

Vol. 1 Selections from *Freedom* 1886-1936
   Supplement: Act For Yourselves! by P. Kropotkin, 20 articles published 1886-1907 and now reprinted for the first time.

Vol. 2 Selections from *Spain and the World* 1936-1939
   Supplement: The May Days: Barcelona 1937

Vol. 3 Selections from *War Commentary / Freedom* 1939-1950
   Supplement: Neither East Nor West, selected writings by Marie Louise Berneri 1939-1948

Vol. 4 Selections from *Freedom* 1951-1964

Vol. 5 A Decade of Anarchy: Selections from the monthly journal *Anarchy* 1961-1970

Vol. 6 Selections from *Freedom* 1965-1986

This ambitious project which has been made financially possible by substantial contributions from FRIENDS OF FREEDOM PRESS LTD. and a long standing friend of FP, Hans Deichmann, should be completed by the end of 1988. All the titles will be available singly in paperback as they are published. Hardback sets will be available. Full particulars from Freedom Press.

MARIE LOUISE BERNERI 1918-1949   photo by V.R

NEITHER EAST NOR WEST
Selected Writings 1939-1948

by
Marie Louise Berneri

with
16 political cartoons 1943-1944
by
John Olday

FREEDOM PRESS
London
1988

Published by
FREEDOM PRESS
84b Whitechapel High Street
London E1 7QX

1988

© Freedom Press

ISBN 0 900384 42 5

PRINTED IN GREAT BRITAIN BY ALDGATE PRESS   LONDON E1 7QX

John Olday (1905-1977) was born in Hamburg, the son of a German mother and a Scottish father. He spent most of his childhood in Hamburg and was at an early age involved in the struggle of the dockworkers there. He left Germany in 1938 and came to this country. When we met him in 1942 at Freedom Press he was in the army and it was the beginning of a collaboration that lasted until 1949, but which was at its most rewarding during the war years. Apart from the cartoons in *War Commentary* and *Freedom*, Freedom Press published in 1943 *The March to Death*, a volume of some 40 anti-war drawings. In 1950 he went to live in Australia, returning to Europe in the late '60s.

Marie Louise Berneri (1918-1949) was born in Arezzo (near Florence) daughter of Giovanna and Camillo. In 1926 they had to flee from persecution by the fascists and she spent the next eleven years in Paris. She came to England in 1937 and was an active member of the Freedom Press group until her untimely death at the age of 31.

EDITOR'S NOTE

The articles comprising this volume were first published in the anarchist journals *War Commentary* (1939-1945) and *Freedom* (1945-)

The Axis and Democracy, Fascists at Work in Algeria, War and Fascism and *Record of the Third International* were written by Marie Louise Berneri in collaboration with John Hewetson; and *The Great Farce of San Francisco, Crisis over Europe, UNO — A Screen for Political Intrigue* and *Does Britain Show the Way* in collaboration with George Woodcock.

CONTENTS

III. UNITED NATIONS

ILLUSTRATIONS
by JOHN OLDAY
1943-1944
Between pages 48-49 and 96-97

EDITOR'S INTRODUCTION

Marie Louise Berneri was an active member of the Freedom Press group from 1937 until her untimely death in 1949 at the age of 31. This selection of her political writings was first published in 1952 by friends as a tribute to her memory.

As editor of the FREEDOM PRESS' Centenary Volume covering the years of *War Commentary* (1939-1945) and its successor *Freedom* up to 1951, I had to decide whether we should reprint these Selections as a Supplement or incorporate some of them into the main volume, the theme of which is contained in the provisional title of *From World War to Cold War*.

Re-reading these articles after thirty-five years I had no hesitation in opting for keeping them together in one volume with the addition of a number of brilliant drawings by John Olday published in *War Commentary* some of which were inspired by Marie Louise Berneri's editorials.

This volume being a supplement to the main volume does not pretend to cover all the major events of those momentous years. Obviously it must be read in conjunction with the other volume. Nevertheless, it has perhaps more relevance in 1988 than it had in 1952 for only now is the Left beginning to question whether World War II was the 'anti-fascist crusade' that they were led to believe it to be — for some a continuation of the 'anti-fascist civil war in Spain'. However, the process of re-thinking that war is a slow one. Certainly the Labour Party hierarchy which joined the nationalist chorus at the time of the Falklands War is not yet ripe for a revision of the Party Line on the 1939 War. Indeed Tony Benn in a recent programme[1] denounced the Falklands War and all the others from the Boer War to Korea and Suez included World War I but made no mention at all of World War II. And at the same time in *Tribune*[2] in an otherwise excellent article: 'Do We Celebrate Needless Slaughter', Peter Tatchell points out that most of the wars this country has been engaged in were for base reasons — markets, raw materials, rival power struggles, etc. . . . but he concludes that

Of the hundred-plus wars fought by Britain since the turn of the century, the Second World War was arguably the only truly just war. In the European theatre, at least, the war was not so much about the defence of Empire as about the right of nations to determine their own future free from fascist *diktat* and for the defence of democratic freedoms, civil liberties and trade union rights which had been hard-won by the European working classes in two centuries of popular struggle.

How naive can one get — or ill-informed, since one has no reason to doubt his integrity. But then he goes on to say

Unfortunately, these noble ideals, which inspired so many British servicemen and women to courageous acts of valour, were quickly extinguished once the war was over. Britain's armed forces were soon turned against our former anti-fascist allies in the Greek partisan resistance and in the Malayan anti-Japanese guerrilla army.

Surely if these are the views of a politically informed writer of the post-war generation it is not surprising to read in *The Independent* at the time of the recent general elections that some critics of Labour's unilateral policy could not understand how the Party trusted the Russians *"after what they had done in the last war"* as though this country had been fighting the Russians in 1939-45!

It will also come as a surprise to those who, through ignorance or in justification for taking sides in a fratricidal war which cost the lives of some fifty million people, to learn that apart from the exceptions, the heroes and heroines referred to by Peter Tatchell, survival was the main concern at all levels of society. Poverty-

1 In the fifth instalment of the Channel 4 programme The Eleventh Hour: The People's Flag, 23 November 1987.
2 13 November 1987 in the feature 'Outwrite'.

stricken farmers in the '30s unable to compete with the food dumped from all over the world suddenly found themselves being treated as VIPs as merchant ships were being regularly sent to the bottom of the ocean. With conscript labour (Women's Land Army) and, later, POWs on the cheap and in spite of rationing, the farmers — like all farmers world-wide have done in similar situations — didn't hand over all their subsidised produce but sold in the black market, and have never looked back. Similarly all the large building and civil engineering firms obtained contracts without tendering — on a cost plus basis — and made fortunes. Similarly for the war industry and suppliers of parts, etc. . . . Is it surprising that the workers ·in industry and vital services felt that they should share in this bonanza — at least get some of the crumbs? It may 'shock' the World War II 'idealists' that there were widespread stoppages in industry and the services: wildcat, unofficial strikes, for the trades union bosses then were working hand-in-glove with the coalition government and the bosses of industry. Olday's cartoon of mid-April 1943 (v. Strikes Increase) shows Ernest Bevin, the Minister of Labour and former Trade Union boss trying to put out the fire aided by the Labour Party (Herbert Morrison) and the Communist Party. Again in mid-March 1944 (x. Strikes Everywhere) Olday contrasts the satisfaction expressed in this country by the government when Italian workers strike against their German oppressors but denounce British strikers. Forty years later we have a Tory government introducing anti-Trades Union legislation in this country while encouraging the Solidarity movement in Poland.

Apart from the books about the campaigns, the politicians the Generals and the Field-Marshalls, it seems to this writer that very little has been written about the cost in human lives. Our historians are still busily exhuming the bones of the victims of Ypres, Verdun and the Somme from the first world war. The post World War II generations in this country have probably heard of the bombing of London and of Coventry, and certainly about the holocaust. Indeed some to whom I have spoken think that the war was declared against Nazi Germany because of the gas chambers, and extermination camps. This is of course not true but is understandable since the

Israel government has not ceased to seek out and bring to trial those involved in the holocaust with full media treatment, whereas no one seeks to bring to trial those who dropped the Atom bombs on Hiroshima and Nagasaki, or the airmen engaged in the block bombing of Italian and German cities and those who ordered these actions.

We know, for example, that the British government, knowing exactly what was happening in Nazi-occupied Europe sought to close the last escape-route down the Danube. In 1943 Lord Cranbourne, the Colonial Secretary wrote to the British ambassador in Turkey to stress that Jews in occupied Europe should not be encouraged to escape, nor should they be organised or helped.[3]

The moral indignation that was generated internationally at top level — for a week or so — when the French National Front leader Le Pen referred to the holocaust as a "minor detail" of the last World War is sheer hypocrisy, just as are Mrs Thatcher's crocodile tears for the innocent victims of Enniskillen when in another context she has publicly declared that she would not hesitate to press the button that could result in the extermination of all human life on this planet.

Of course the holocaust was not a *detail* but the most horrific of the many *horrors that are unleashed by War*. Section 2 of these Selections *The Price of War and of Liberation*, and Olday's cartoons bring this out forcefully, for we need to be reminded of the fact that the last war involved not only the military but for the first time civilians on a massive scale. War is legalised terrorism. The victims are the innocent on both sides. The top guilty are either hanged or ennobled and decorated depending on which side wins.

In the very week that the Media and all the Party leaders were beating their breasts over the civilian victims at the Enniskillen War Memorial ceremony the *Sunday Telegraph* (November 14 1987) was

---

3 The Channel 4 Documentary on *Raoul Wallenberg: Between the Lines* (26 November 1987) made it quite clear that thousands of Hungarian and other Jews died because the "democracies" were not interested in saving them. For instance the programme revealed that in the decade to 1943 the United States gave refuge to only 10 per cent of the number that they were allowed by law, leaving 400,000 places unfilled within the quota.

publishing a letter from a (Flt Lt) F.C.A. Lanning (Rtd) of Darlington on the subject of the bombing of Hamburg in which he writes:

Referring to a recent self-pitying German documentary on the bombing of Hamburg in 1943, your correspondent Evelyn Dunford seems surprised that your commentator Daniel Johnson should have contrasted the bitterness of the survivors with the phlegmatic, businesslike manner of the surviving Allied aircrew members who also appeared in the documentary.

Believe me, any airman who had witnessed what the Germans did to London, Coventry and other cities two years previously, at a time when *Bomben über England* was the most popular song in Germany, could not fail to look phlegmatic and businesslike at the proud memory of having participated in the delivery of a copious dose of the bully's own medicine right on his very own doorstep![4]

Marie Louise Berneri had every reason to feel bitter about the Communists, but her criticisms are always carefully documented and therefore valuable for anyone today honestly seeking to make an objective assessment of the changes that have taken place in the Soviet Union more especially in the present phase of its development. In the last article, *Neither East nor West* written at the end of 1947 she made her position crystal clear (page 187)

We now have the appeasers of Russia. They are so hypnotised by the vision of atomic war that they are prepared to turn a blind eye on crimes committed under their very noses.

We wholly disagree with this attitude. We do not think that war can be avoided by a policy which entails the suppression of facts. We hold this view for ethical reasons, but also for practical ones. Ethical: because we do not believe in suppressing truth to suit a certain policy; this would be propaganda in the pejorative sense which our correspondent gives to that word. We are not interested in "propaganda". We denounced the Russian

---

4 Unlike the Fl Lt (Rtd) and his companions who feel no shame for their part in the terror bombing of German civilians a number of Australian former air pilots involved in the block bombing of Germans declared that they had not been able to live at peace with themselves ever since.

régime during the war at a time when everybody was praising Stalin, from Mr. Churchill downwards. If we are concerned in furthering "capitalist propaganda" we would not have chosen to say unpopular truths all these years.

We cannot alter our views about Russia simply because, for imperialist reasons, American and British spokesmen now denounce Russian totalitarianism. We know that their indignation is hypocritical and that they may become friendly to Russia again if it suits their interests. But for all that, are we to stifle our own indignation?

Apart from the ex-Communists who are the most vocal denouncers of their God(s) that Failed, many anarchists because of the persecution of their comrades under Lenin and Stalin, as well as the reactionary and terrorist role played by the Stalinist regime internationally, and especially in destroying the revolutionary élan in Spain in 1937[5] cannot see or admit that there have been changes which anarchists should be studying and appraising. I am quite convinced that had our comrade lived to observe what was happening in the Soviet Union she certainly would not have joined the "appeasers" but at least would have recognised that something must be rumbling *from below* to explain the reforms being introduced *from above*, just as surely as she would have sought an explanation for Thatcherism in this country in the "corrupting" effect of the consumerist society on the workers' organisations.

Her description of the *United Nations* in Section 3 as "A Screen for Political Intrigue" (p.139) is as true today as it was forty years ago.

The United Nations and all its ramifications are undoubtedly the world's largest Multinational industry employing directly and indirectly millions of people, from the top politicians and civil servants via the specialists (economists, scientists, academics, you name them) through the interpreters, the hostesses, the personal secretaries and the speech writers to the media hacks whose very existence depends on the "crises", the hand-outs and — for the most sychophantic — the "inspired leaks". And at the end of it all South Africa's white boors go on persecuting and exploiting the blacks;

5 See May Days in Barcelona 1937 (Freedom Press 1987)

Russian conscripts go on dying in Afghanistan as do the American financed Rebels; Iran and Iraq go on decimating their Youth while upstarts worldwide continue to declare themselves the saviours of their countries; Thatcher dismisses the overwhelming majority that says Britain and Argentina must settle their differences while Gore Vidal accuses the USA of being the most Imperialist nation of the Twentieth Century . . . to a world opinion that is deaf.

Yet another reason for keeping these articles together as a volume. Re-reading them after so many years I feel they are an example of anarchistic journalism at its best. They burn with the passion and indignation of a young revolutionary in her twenties *avec le diable au corps* combined with self-control, irony and a cool marshalling of her facts. Today much of the indignation is expressed by four-letter expletives, chaotic graphics and horrific drawings. I think also that Marie Louise Berneri's generation — and especially on the Continent — were much more politically informed and involved in knowing what was going on on the Left and this is reflected in the many quotations and references. One should of course add that forty years ago newspapers were actually publishing news.[6] Today like the popular take-away foods, they serve up the news processed and artificially flavoured by a mafia of columnists who — unlike the James Camerons of the past — hack away for the highest bidder.

Lastly, but of importance for the reader, is Marie Louise's family background. Briefly then, since I refer to it in the 1952 *Foreword*. She and her family were, in the first place, victims of the fascist regime in Italy who in 1926 were obliged to go into exile when she was eight years old. She grew up in Paris in an atmosphere of constant harassment by the French authorities of the anti-fascist refugees and especially of her father Camillo Berneri who was

---

6 This was startlingly revealed in November 1987 when the *Guardian* commemmorated the Russian Revolution by including for the week a page in facsimile of the *Manchester Guardian* for 1917. No gimmicks by the layout man. Solid columns of factual material broken up into fifty or more items with a one column headline.

regularly arrested by the French who would then hand him over to the Belgians who would also seek to get rid of him and this went on until the Spanish Civil War when he joined the struggle in Catalonia ending in assassination by the Communists during the May Days, Barcelona 1937.

And from London (her home from 1937) she learned in 1940 that her mother, who had been active, especially after the death of Camillo, dealing with the Spanish refugees as well as the Italians, had been arrested by the French police and handed over to the Italian fascist authorities via German and Austrian prisons, and only had news after the "liberation" of Italy.

So any critic of this volume who would dismiss it on the grounds that the writer had lived a sheltered life and didn't know what fascism was all about, must look for better arguments!

Colchester November 1987   *VERNON RICHARDS*

FOREWORD

Hundreds of books on various aspects of the second world war have appeared during the past seven years of "peace". Most have come from the pens of leading politicians, soldiers and journalists. Few have come from the lower ranks, and, so far as we know, no autobiographies, or diaries by private soldiers who fought at the fronts have yet appeared in print. Some of the books published have sought to exploit the "glorious" side of war; the heroism and solidarity, and the daring attempts to escape from prison camps. It is not surprising that in our society these books should prove to be publishers' best sellers, and sure successes for film producers. As for the authors among the politicians and generals one notes a significant discrepancy in their accounts and interpretations of the military and political events of the war years. Indeed, one is bound to suspect the objectivity of such histories which, quite apart from their absence of self-criticism, seem also to be influenced by the geographical location of their authors.

A third category of post war volumes is that of books aimed at whitewashing some of the most sinister political and military figures of our time. Sometimes they whitewash themselves (the Ciano and Laval diaries, for example), on other occasions it is done for them (Rommel, Pétain).

All these "histories" of the war, or aspects of it, owe their popularity not necessarily to their objectivity: not because they attempt to draw moral lessons from the experience of war, nor because they denounce war and conclude, as the Director-General of the United Nations World Health Organisation did recently, that war must be "discarded" as an "obsolete behaviour pattern". No, they owe their popularity to the reader's hope or to the publisher's assurance, that their authors have revealed some new sensational facts. And who could possibly afford to miss any scandal among the high-ups? This latent "witch-hunt" spirit in a large section of the public, coupled with high pressure "promotion" by the publishers seem to sell these books as fast as each new title appears on the market. It is obviously a profitable business for all who take part in it. But the real value of all these books will be seen in a few years time, for there is no reason to doubt that their ultimate fate will be any different from the large majority of similar books published after the first world war, which, when they escape the rag and bone man, clutter up the six-penny shelves of secondhand bookstalls, or vie with travellers reminiscences as the mainstay of the libraries in our prisons.

This first collection of the late Marie Louise Berneri's articles contains no sensational revelations which will assure vast sales for it. Even the title is an accurate description of the subject matter of the book. What is "sensational" about this book is the fact that it is, to our knowledge, the only work in print in which the author takes up an uncompromising position in opposition to both the Western Powers and their hangers-on, and the Soviet Union and its satellites.

It is, indeed, a sad comment on the bankruptcy of the International Labour Movement, that in the space of less than forty years only the small anarchist movements and a few socialist groups maintain the traditional opposition of the working classes to all wars, in which they are always the victims, and the losers. With the last war, the leaders of the Labour movement for the first time unanimously spoke of the "ideological war". What, in fact had changed since 1914-18? The old ruling class have referred to all wars as "wars for Freedom", "wars to end wars". For them, the nature of wars is the same to-day as it was in the past. What has changed is the Labour movement—or rather the Leadership of that movement. From a rank and file movement, struggling against the injustices of the boss and the Government, indeed against the capitalist system, it has grown into a vast organisation—in numbers, financially, and in the power it wields—controlled by an army of bureaucrats and politicians, intent on winning and holding power. But power they now tell us, brings with it responsibility and wisdom. Just as the hierarchy of pigs in *Animal Farm* in the end saw the enemy's point of view so well that one could not distinguish the pigs from the humans, so the Labour politicians, as Marie Louise Berneri points out, assume power by "adopting the policy of the Right". In other words what has happened during the past forty years is not that the *nature* of war has changed, but that the Labour politicians have with their rise to power, changed sides.

At one time they prided themselves on their internationalism. To-day they do not even bother to conceal their nationalism; *plus roi que le roi* can well be applied to the Labour Party leadership to-day.* And, as M. L. Berneri wrote in dealing with the British Army of Oppression in Asia, "The Labour Government has shown that it will pursue an imperialist policy worthy of any Tory Government. The Trade Union Congress in Paris has shown that the Trade Unions of the home countries share the imperialist aims of their governments and look with hostility on the Trade Unions of colonial countries when these show aspirations towards independence" (p. 128).

The first thing that this volume sets out to do is to lay bare the pretence that the last war was ever an ideological struggle between the forces of democracy on the one side and the evil forces of fascism on the other. Marie Louise Berneri was not wise *after* the event as are so many present critics of the last war, but wrote the articles comprising the first section of this book between 1941 and 1943.

To those who read the pages that follow with an open and inquiring mind, the second and third sections are surely a warning that just as the last war was not a struggle between fascism and anti-fascism, so the present cold war, or any future one, is not, and will not be an ideological war between democracy and totalitarianism. Nowhere will one find Marie Louise Berneri minimising the dangers, inherent in Stalinism, to all the human values which were dear to her. But "this conviction—she wrote in 1947—does not lead us to seek refuge in the arms of British or American Imperialism. We realize, on the contrary that Russia's strength lies in the fact that her only opponents are as corrupted and ruthless as she is herself. As long as Socialists and other Leftists go on fighting Communism by hiding behind America's skirts they are bound to be defeated". How "corrupted and ruthless" are Russia's opponents has become

---

*How far the leadership has travelled is contained in that memorable sentence uttered by the leader of the Labour Party, ex-Premier Clement Attlee, on the occasion of the death of George VI: "The longer I served him the greater was my admiration, respect and affection. No Prime Minister had a kinder or more considerate master".

during the past two years so evident that even some of the prominent
radicals who had unconditionally surrendered to America as the only
answer to the "Russian menace" are now having second thoughts.

It is a view put forward and encouraged, for obvious reasons, by
politicians of the West that the totalitarian régimes are firmly en-
trenched and that the people in these countries blindly go to their
death at the least order from their leaders. Quite apart from the fact
that these arguments create the false impression that in our democracies *we* tell our leaders what to do, there is no evidence to show that
the masses in the totalitarian countries are any more gullible than
those in the West.

Mussolini's dictatorship revealed that it had feet of clay. It may
be true that the final push to his régime was given by the Allied
armies, but the fact remains that long before this the Italian soldiers
had shown clearly that they had no intention of fighting to defend it.
We now know, from the Ciano diaries and other documents that the
régime was far from homogeneous, and that a struggle for power was
going on all the time. Again, from the article on terror trials in Jugoslavia written in March 1947, we learn that the victims were
Jehovah's Witnesses accused of spying for the *Americans* against the
"new democracies". But by 1949 Tito's courts were trying Communists accused of spying for *Russia,* and his Government was receiving financial and military aid from America and Britain! In the
series of articles on the seizure of power by the Communists in
Czechoslovakia written in 1947-48 (incidentally, how much more in-
sight M. L. Berneri showed into political developments in that
country than did the professional journalists and politicians) one
comes across names of Communist leaders who were responsible for
liquidating social democrats and who by 1952 are themselves either
among the liquidated or awaiting liquidation. There is indeed,
abundant evidence of a struggle for power in the Communist countries
which cannot be ignored in assessing the stability of these régimes.

There emerges too, we think, from a reading of this volume the
author's utter objectivity, but never any signs of indifference, or lack
of humanity. Nationalism had no place in her thought. As she
summed up the position herself: "We shall denounce political trials
whether they are held in Washington or Warsaw. When a Govern-

ment puts a man in jail for his political opinions, we do not ask the
nationality of that government. We are always on the side of the
victim of State tyranny". And again, we recall that when she took
up the cause of a group of Spanish P.O.W.s who were interned in
Chorley, Lancs., her sense of the injustice of which they were victims
was stronger than any personal feelings she might have had that
among these men were a number of Communists—supporters of the
assassins of her father, Camillo Berneri, in Barcelona during the May
Days of 1937.

Marie Louise Berneri's objectivity should be an example to the
intelligentsia of the Left who in 1939 supported the war because they
feared the concentration camps if the Nazis won. (What a godsend
was the "captured" Nazi Black List of Englishmen destined for the
concentration camp!) Now there is almost hysterical personal fear
of Russia. (And we do not doubt that the Communist Parties
throughout the world have their lists ready for when the time comes.
But then so have the Americans who have also, with their customary
thoroughness, prepared four concentration camps to receive the
victims!)

Marie Louise Berneri was never influenced in her judgments
by personal considerations, though, with her family, she had
lived under fascism, had experienced the life of a refugee in a reactionary France, had lost her father in Spain at the hands of Communist gunmen, had lived through the anxiety of knowing that her
mother had been arrested in Paris by the Gestapo after the fall of
France in 1940, and that the same fate might have befallen her sister
and many close friends.

She spent all the war years in London, and not even her prosecution with three of her comrades, which threatened penalties of up to
14 years imprisonment, deflected her from her course in writing and
saying publicly what she thought was right.

A Spanish anarchist has written elsewhere* of the way she was
deeply shocked by the attitude of those Spanish refugees who supported
the last war simply on the tactical grounds than an allied victory
would mean the overthrow of Franco and their subsequent return to
their homes and families in Spain.

*In an appreciation contributed by a Spanish refugee to the memorial
volume: *Marie Louise Berneri, 1918-1949. A Tribute.* Freedom Press,
1949.

How the intellectual honesty, which emerges from such a
position as she adopted coupled with her burning indignation against
injustice, whether it occurred in defeated Germany or defenceless
Burma, compare with the rascality of the politicians who denounced
the Nazi concentration camps only when they were at war with
Germany; who conveniently forgot about slave labour in Russia
during the war years when they were allies, only to re-discover it now
that they are brothers in arms no longer ; who now declare that
Franco, with so many thousands of lives on his conscience, is really
the leading democrat in Europe since he has been fighting "communism" longer than anybody else; and who now whitewash Tito's
totalitarian régime because he has broken with Stalin!

It is this political opportunism, cynicism and hypocrisy that Marie
Louise Berneri denounced with all her energy and intelligence during
her all too short life.   And if this volume of her writings did no more
than this, it will have justified its publication to-day.   But we think
it also offers something more directly positive: it is a plea for real
internationalism among ordinary men and women, and for a humanism,
and sense of human dignity as the guiding principle in our lives.
This is surely what she meant when she wrote: "We refuse to accept
the statement that the trials which are now taking place in Europe
should not concern us.   It is true that our protests will not change
the course of events, *but we must voice them nevertheless* . . . " (our
italics).   For her it was impossible to stand by and watch an injustice
being perpetrated: to do so was to forfeit one's self-respect and dignity
as a human being.

Imperialism is not a *new* threat to civilisation.   The new danger
is that the propaganda of a life or death choice between West and East
is fostering the general acceptance of Machiavelian principles and a
justification of the means by the end, at the expense of the radical
principle that "an injury to one is the concern of all".   Marie Louise
Berneri belonged to that small band of uncompromising defenders
of our social conscience, as her writings bear witness.   Because of
this they will still be valuable when the events she discusses in them
have ceased to be of any topical interest.

London, April 1952.   V.R.

A Constructive Policy

WE ARE often accused of lacking a constructive policy. People grant
that we have made a valuable analysis of the present situation, and
that "our paper has a real value in pricking complacency and stimulating thought". But we are asked to put forward "practical" solutions
for the struggle against fascism and capitalism.

Needless to say we do not accept the charges made against us.
We admit that our readers will not find in our pages prescriptions for
curing humanity from all the ills that beset it. What some of our
readers obviously would like are slogans, manifestos, and programmes
which offer to the working-class in a few lines the means of achieving
not only the end of fascism but also of bringing about the era of
workers' happiness.

We refuse to adopt such recipe-programmes because we are convinced that the present weakness of the working-class is due to the
fact that every party, in order to gain popularity and power, has
simplified its programmes, reducing to ridiculous proportions the
nature of the struggle that will bring freedom to the exploited.

Political slogans have become like patent medicine advertisements
promising health, beauty, and happiness in exchange for a tablet of
soap, or a cup of cocoa. Vote Labour, and everything will be all
right! Pay your trade union dues and security will be assured! A
workers' government will achieve the revolution! Write to your
M.P. or to such-and-such a Minister, march through the streets in
a disciplined manner, with a powerful band and shout till you're
hoarse, and all your wishes (demands) will be granted!

That is what parties alleged to have a "realist" policy and holding
in the greatest contempt the "anarchist Utopians", have been advocating for a quarter of a century whenever a difficulty arose. These
remedies have proved useless against unemployment and fascism,

Italian aggression in Abyssinia, Anglo-French boycott of the Spanish revolutionaries, rearmament and war. And yet the same methods are again advanced to meet the problems created by the present situation.

The leit-motiv of left parties is that the workers should take as much control as they can of the government. This appears constructive enough. But it only means that Labour leaders will enter the Government by adopting the policy of the Right. For the workers it means sacrifices and the loss of every kind of liberty in order to secure the privilege of seeing "their" Ministers sitting on the Cabinet benches. No improvements are obtained and all official channels for making discontent heard are lost.

Another "practical" solution advocated by the Labour Party is to issue a declaration of war or peace aims. Apparently the world should know of our love of freedom and justice. May we "utopians" suggest to the editorial board of the *Daily Herald* that if the Labour Party is anxious to show the world how "democratic" we are, it could for instance refuse to be associated with a government which imprisons Nehru for four years (may we add that petitions, open letters, etc., etc., will not have the slightest effect?).

It is not by changing ministers—such guilty men!—or issuing declarations that fascism and capitalism will be conquered. The problem is more complex than that. We do not intend to add our voice to those who delude the workers that their "leaders" will get them out of the mess. The problems need a complete transformation in the present attitude of the working class. You cannot change the present régime while there is no revolutionary spirit, while the workers will not understand a few fundamental truths.

1. That workers and capitalists cannot have a common cause.
2. That imperialism is the prime cause of war, and the cause must be eradicated.
3. That governments, Tory and Labour, are always instruments of oppression, and that the workers must learn to do without them.
4. That parties seek power only for their own benefit—a small minority. Therefore all power must be seized and retained in the hands of syndicates which comprise the great majority of the men and women producers.

We cannot build until the working class gets rid of its illusions, its acceptance of bosses and faith in leaders. Our policy consists in educating it, in stimulating its class instinct, and teaching methods of struggle. It is a hard and long task, but to the people who prefer such expedient solutions as war, we would point out that the great world war which was to end war and safeguard democracy, only produced fascism and another war; that this war will doubtless produce other wars, while leaving untouched the underlying problems of the workers. Our way of refusing to attempt the futile task of patching up a rotten world, but of striving to build a new one, is not only constructive but is also the *only* way out.

December, 1940.

1

Defenders of Democracy

---

1. WILL AMERICA RULE THE WORLD?

MR. ROOSEVELT seems to have stepped into the shoes of the Almighty. From all sides come flattering greetings and most urgent requests. These requests do not reach him from rulers of the world only but also from the pens of pacifists and socialists. In *Peace News*, for instance, it has been suggested that it is up to Roosevelt to call a conference to end the war, and the Editor of *Forward*, having apparently lost hope since the end of September of hearing King George VI announce over the radio that peace had been made with Germany, suggested, on October 28th, "an International Peace Conference to be called immediately to be held in the U.S.A., under the presidency of President Roosevelt . . . "

A naive observer may well ask himself what are the qualifications of the President of the United States to justify such universal confidence. Roosevelt's moving appeals which have reached Europe during the last few years have been strangely contradicted by his eagerness to turn the war to profit as soon as it was declared. Thanks to this great pacifist, Wall Street is rubbing its hands at the prospect of French and English orders, and the importance given, during the debate on the Neutrality Act to the cash and carry provision leaves no doubt as to the disinterested sympathies of the U.S. for the two democracies!

The *Star* of Kansas City puts it in a nutshell: "Plain commonsense and national interests require this country to throw open all its resources to the nations who come to buy American goods of whatever sort." Furthermore it has been "estimated by a Government economist that between 1,000,000 and 1,500,000 of America's unemployed will obtain jobs by January if war brings large foreign orders and stimulates more intensive investment of private capital." The economic situation in America can **hardly be called bright at** the present time. She needs new markets for her products; the New Deal has not met with the success hoped for and the war may just bring the prosperity to increase Roosevelt's popularity.

The United States are ruled by capitalist interests (probably to a greater extent than any other country) and these interests seem to identify themselves with American imperialist interests. In fact, one can justly ask whether, from an imperialist point of view, the United States have not a great deal to gain by a war which will weaken their three great rivals: Germany, Britain and France. No matter where the United States have attempted to establish their domination, whether in Asia or the Americas, they have always clashed with British or German interests.

In China, British interests are more extensive than American interests. Whereas Britain owns the banks, railways and mines, America, who arrived on the scene later, has the monopoly in aviation and only a few investments in the mines and railways. Even in these, they clash with German interests.

In Latin America the conflict between European powers and the U.S. is no less noticeable. It was manifest recently in regard to the nationalisation of the Mexican petroleum companies, the outcome of which, has been a victory for American interests. As the *Bulletin of the Archives of Geneva*, dated the 7th of June, points out:

"From now onward, the United States is the indisputable master of all the domains of Mexico. The last British stronghold (in Latin America) has been demolished to its foundations. The United States have employed the only means of driving the English from Mexico without firing a single shot."

It is also suggested in the *Bulletin* that it was with the aid of Cardenas that the English were finally driven out of Mexico. This was accomplished without difficulty. While the English were rejoicing in the possession of 60 per cent. of the petrol in Mexico as opposed to the 40 per cent. controlled by the American companies, Cardenas expropriated it all. But, while the expropriation aroused a storm of indignation in London, it was greeted calmly in Washington. What would that suggest? According to the *Bulletin*, an understanding was reached between Washington and Mexico by which all the petrol would be American "thus demolishing the last British stronghold in this hemisphere".

And a recent report which appeared in the *Daily Telegraph*, (26/11/39), states that the Mexican petrol has been sold to an "Independent American firm".

In South America, too, the dreams of American hegemony have been baldy jarred by German propaganda in recent years, and no doubt the U.S. would welcome the removal of such a dangerous rival.

Is it too much to suggest that the United States have the opportunity of gradually ousting Britain, even in the Dominion markets, due to the increasing difficulties created by the war on production and transport from the Metropolis?

Let it not be said that the above is pure Machiavellism and that American opinion, and perhaps Roosevelt himself, do not experience a genuine sympathy for the democracies. The opinions of the masses (or rather, what the press makes them believe) has nothing in common with the combined capitalist and imperialist interests which determine the policy of the country. But it must be recognised that these interests have everything to gain by a European war. And if it is as yet too early to forecast accurately the results of this war, one can however state that the United States by promising help to the democracies, and Russia by promising help to Germany, are ready to reap the fruits of their cunning political manœuvres.

December, 1939.

2. AMERICAN IMPERIALISM *versus* GERMAN IMPERIALISM

Woodrow Wilson, in his message to Congress in 1917, said, "The world must be made safe for Democracy. America is privileged to shed her blood for the principles that gave her birth."

Walter H. Page, U.S. Ambassador to Great Britain, in a cable to Wilson on March 5th, 1917, one month before America entered the war, said, "The pressure of the approaching crisis has gone beyond the ability of the Morgan Financial Agency. The only way of maintaining our pre-eminent trade position is by declaring war on Germany."

Now THAT President Roosevelt enters his third term and that the fever of the elections is over the United States can dedicate themselves wholeheartedly to their vast rearmament programme. Those measures are apparently intended to prevent war just as war preparations are supposed to stop war in France and England. But when a country arms itself to the teeth, conscripts its men, organises its production according to war needs it is folly to hope that war will not follow. The U.S.A. seems to come every day nearer the moment when they will be involved in conflict with German and Japanese imperialism. If the struggle has not started yet it is because conflicting interests cause American indecision. The situation is similar to that of Britain before the war. It was obvious that in the long run German imperialism would clash with the British. But the policy of democratic imperialism is always a short term one. A long term policy would mean sacrificing in part the immediate interests of the capitalists for the interests of capitalism as a whole. This was not done. That is why iron ore and machinery were sent to Germany, loans were made which allowed them to rearm, etc. In the same way the interests of the capitalists in the U.S. pursuing a short term policy do not come into conflict with the interests of German imperialism. England menaced them to a much greater extent and this fact explains the indecision in American policy during the last few years, and even now. In spite of the fact that Japan, for example, is considered as a potential enemy she has received from America ample supplies of oil and scrap iron. In spite of the sympathy for England a blockade of material going to Germany has not been made effective, as is shown by the enormous increase of exports to neutral countries such as Russia for example.*

However the recent German victories oblige America to take a less immediately profitable, but, in the long run, wiser policy. They seem to realize now that an arrangement between German and American imperialisms is impossible. Germany will never conform to the

*Other examples could be given of American support for the German air industry (see *Left* for October, 1940).

rules of the imperialist game as England, for example, did. Its economic structure is too different from the American for the compromise to be made. Germany disregards the most fundamental rule —that of the respect due to gold. They discovered (they were forced to) that a nation, in order to gain the respect of the world, had less need of immense reserves of gold than of a powerful army and a centralized economy; that an efficient ministry of propaganda could obtain better results than a bank director with loans.

Such a conception cannot be too popular in a country which possesses about 80 per cent. of the world's gold reserve. The last world war had already increased considerably American gold reserves. From a debtor country it became the largest creditor in the whole world. Since the beginning of this war European gold has gone to increase this gold reserve still further. During the first seven months it increased by 11 per cent. On July 25th it amounted to 20,400,000,000 dollars worth of monetary gold (*Times*) and this does not include the foreign gold put in safety in the U.S.A. What is to be done with that immense quantity of gold hoarded in the mountains of Kentucky? How can it be put into circulation again? Various remedies have been proposed, such as that of M. Van Zeeland, for the redistribution of gold. But this redistribution can only be made by credit and it would impose an unbearable burden on the countries which would have to accept it, *i.e.* those which have suffered most in the war. The economic situation of the European countries after the war will be such that they will have little enough products to exchange against American gold.

The Treasury secretary Mr. Morgenthau declared last year that the immense reserves of gold possessed by the U.S. will allow them to undertake the rôle which they ought to play in the reconstruction of the world, which must follow the mad destruction of the war. "Reconstruction" meaning investment of capital, for it is obvious that the only solution for America would be to lend her gold and to make the whole world her debtor. But "reconstruction" could be markedly hampered by German competition. If Hitler dominates Europe gold will find no employment there, nor in the countries under German influence outside Europe where the method of barter employed in Central Europe would probably be adopted. If Japan follows in Germany's footsteps America will find it difficult to employ her gold and the world will run the risk of being swamped with American gold watches in the same way as it has been with German aspirins!

The present rearmament programme will, however, thanks to the great expense involved, partly solve the American problem by starting a redistribution of the gold reserves. At the same time it will provide America with the necessary military strength to allow her to help in the "reconstruction" of the post-war world.

Diplomacy and propaganda are the other means used to increase her sphere of influence. The first to fall under her protection are of course the countries of South America and Mexico. "Under cover of the 'good neighbour' policy and the 'defence' of Latin-America against fascism, Uncle Sam is cracking the whip over Mexico, and the new Camacho régime there shows every sign of capitulation", says the American journal *The Call* (2/11/40) and adds:

"The whip being used over the backs of the Mexican people is the $500,000,000 loan which is being dispensed in Latin-America through the U.S. Export-Import bank. Without settlement of the oil controversy on terms 'satisfactory' to American oil firms—which means reimbursements of those interests which have drained Mexico's resources for years—the State Department has made it clear that U.S. loans would not be forthcoming.

It is obvious, however, that the State Department's interest in Mexico at the moment does not stop with its concern for the profits of American oil firms. The United States is exacting a political as well as a monetary price for its paternalism. The basic aim of the State Department is to force Avila Camacho (who is far more of an opportunist politician than Cardenas ever was) far to the right of the radical reform program instituted by Cardenas. Its real aim is to undermine the Mexican Revolution, making Mexico safe for American exploitation and a strong link in the American imperialist system. The finishing touches are expected to be put on this job when Camacho visits the United States shortly after the U.S. elections."

Another means of obtaining the surrender of Camacho was the boycott of Mexican oil. The U.S. government refused to buy the petrol from the American companies selling Mexican oil in spite of the fact that they were selling it at a cheaper price than the Standard

Oil opponents of the Mexican government. Left without a market for its petrol the Mexican government had to make peace with Standard Oil on its terms.

Intrigue was also used. After the elections the U.S.A. harboured Almazan the Mexican fascist candidate who pretended that the elections had been rigged to his disadvantage. In the U.S. he proclaimed his right to the presidentship and provoked sedition in Mexico. The American press exaggerated these reports so as to make out that Camacho's régime was in danger. But when Camacho in fright gave in, all agitation ceased, Almazan renounced his aspirations and returned to Mexico the same day as Henry A. Wallace the American envoy arrived.

Employing methods similar to those that Germany used in order to arm herself against British Imperialism, America prepares to crush her rivals. The clash between the old form of imperialism represented by the United States and the new represented by Germany and Japan seems inevitable. Only the abandonment of both forms of imperialism can prevent it. Will the working class be able to impose their will?

February, 1941.

3. THE AXIS *versus* "DEMOCRACY"

JAPAN'S AGGRESSION in Indo-China has been described in the capitalist press as threatening British and American interests in the Far East. The threat must obviously be greater now than formerly, since the British and American Governments have judged it necessary to take drastic steps, such as the freezing of all Japanese credits and the bringing of "all financial and trade export transactions in which Japanese interests are involved under the control of the Government" (White House Statement). The U.S. Government seems to be willing to go to the length of actually imposing an embargo on all important materials. "The nature of the White House announcement made it appear that the operations would be conducted so as to bar Japan from vital sources of oil, petrol and other war materials" (*Daily Telegraph*, 26/7/41).

It is very interesting to note the reaction of the British and American Governments to this new move of Japan's. When China was invaded and the Chinese people bombed and starved to death, there was a great deal of talk about poor democratic China being invaded and pillaged by aggressive Japan. The Governments of the democracies openly declared their moral support for China, and their strong disapproval of the yellow partner of the Axis. It will be said that more than merely moral support was afforded to China in the shape of loans; but that was simply conscience money from the profits made by selling goods to Japan, as we shall see later. The conflict had to go on or business would have stopped.

However, now that Japan represents a plain threat to "our" territories, the attitude of the democracies becomes rather more realistic. Instead of so much mere talk about Fascism *versus* Democracy, active steps are taken. To-day it is openly admitted that Japan could not make war without British and American aid:

"In the economic field Anglo-American retaliation can be made deadly. A recent Japanese envoy extraordinary to Latin-America pleaded that access to petroleum was imperative for Japan's war on China. Ninety per cent. of the oil Japan burns must come from abroad, and two-thirds of it have been coming from the United States, with the rest from British Malaya and the Dutch East Indies. Co-operative retaliatory measures could therefore leave Japan with practically nothing but her stocks to sustain the Chinese war and supply the forces she is sending to Indo-China and her fleet. From the United States and the British Empire, too, she has been obtaining some four-fifths of the iron and steel and rubber essential to modern warfare. Drastic enforcement of sanctions on her imports would not have to be long sustained to bring her industries to a standstill. It remains to be seen whether the militarists of Tokyo have counted the cost of challenging the greatest producing and the greatest industrial States of the world" (*Daily Telegraph*, July 26th, 1941).

When hypocritical tears were shed over democratic China by our Government and the Labour Party, we were not impressed. We pointed out that the conflict was only made possible with British and American collaboration. At that time capitalists in both countries thought a war between China and Japan more profitable to them than a free China. They now seem to think that Japan has gone too far, and they have to sacrifice a little to save much. As long as they admit that they are only defending "their" interests it is all right. But the workers' interests have nothing in common with these, and when they are told that it is another war for democracy, they will know that it is just another lie.

August, 1941.

4. "DEMOCRATIC" RUSSIA

ROOSEVELT DESCRIBED Russia last May as being in the totalitarian bloc in the great division of the world into "blacks" and "whites". Since then Stalin's entry into the war alongside the Allies has given rise to the most fantastic and ridiculous contradictions in the ideological cover imparted to the war by the partisans of "democracy". Of course, democracy had already been made to embrace anti-semitic and near-Fascist Poland and the Greek dictatorship, while overtures were made to a dictatorial Turkey and clerical-Fascist Spain (not to mention those extended to Mussolini's Italy in the early months of the war). But "democratic" Russia is a tougher piece to swallow. Meanwhile gallant little Finland has to be regarded in an altered light also.

Not so long ago, the most reactionary propagandists used to fulminate about the war of freedom *versus* dictatorship, and imply that Stalin was even worse than Hitler; all that is changed now. The papers that used to condemn "godless Moscow", now front-page the reports of the Patriarch and the Muscovites praying for victory. The Bolsheviks and their Red Army, hitherto gleefully described as hopelessly inefficient, are now soberly praised for their "ruthless efficiency and determination", etc. Those who could hardly find words to express their contempt for the Nazis' cowardly policy of scuttling their vessels, loudly extol the essentially similar Russian policy of "scorched earth". Meanwhile Hitler has also had to reverse his home propaganda as well. In short, the whole lamentable farce of justificatory propaganda on both sides has had to be cynically reversed.

The capitalist Press, as a whole, has not, however, followed up the B.B.C.'s attempt of June 22nd to present Russia as a democracy. Even the *New Statesman*, in its editorial comment on Bernard Shaw's letter (31st May, 1941), points to the futility of that view. " . . . but to deny that Stalin is a dictator makes nonsense of this realistic defence . . . etc.", and they emphasised in a later issue the "spiritual gulf" between Russia and Great Britain. The attitude of the capitalist Press is well summarized in this extract from the *New Statesman* for June 28th: "The Government must use the chance to remedy these inefficiencies (*i.e.*, in war production) and the fact that the Soviet Union, which in the minds of millions remains the symbol of the workers' state, is now fighting on the same side as ourselves against a common enemy, should have an electric effect in the factories and workshops." In other words, the *New Statesman*, together with the rest of the capitalist Press, is not deceived, but they are quite ready to exploit the illusions of the workers regarding Russia. And, as usual, the left wing Press renders them invaluable assistance in maintaining the illusion that the U.S.S.R. is a workers' state.

The Social Democrats seem to be divided on the alleged central issue of the war—Democracy *versus* Dictatorship—though, of all people, they should know where democracy really exists. Some have sided with (what are generally called) the Axis Powers, others with (what are generally assumed to be) Democracies.

The Swedish Coalition Government, with the Social-Democratic Prime Minister, is more anti-Russian than anti-Nazi. "It has allowed German troops to pass through Sweden, and now it is encouraging men to apply for postponement of military service in order to enrol in the Finnish Army. The Defence Minister says that such applications will be received 'benevolently'." (*The New Leader*, 12/7/41). It will be remembered that Sweden organized a corps of volunteers to fight for Finland in the Russo-Finnish war. The Swedish Left Socialist Party, on the other hand, takes the contrary view that an Allied victory is preferable to a German one . . .

Meanwhile the Finnish Labour Movement, so loudly praised in the British Press eighteen months ago, also supports the Nazis against Russia. "Mr. Tanner, the Labour leader, has joined the

Government as Minister of Trade and Industry. 'The workers of Finland', he states, 'will least of all have cause to mourn if the Soviet régime breaks.. In this matter our interests run common with those of Germany, which is now attacking the Soviet Union'." (*New Leader,* 12/7/41). In recalling Citrine's "My Finnish Diary", comment would be superfluous.

Adam Ciolkoscz, the Secretary of the Polish Socialist Party, declares, in a letter disagreeing with the *New Leader*'s policy regarding Russia, that the Polish Social Democrats consider themselves still at war with Russia. (The "Free" Polish Government of General Sikorski, meanwhile, is now negotiating a "peace" with the Kremlin, after having been at war with Russia since September, 1939!) Truly, the Second International of to-day, is worthily living up to the example of its leaders in the last war!

August, 1941.

5. "AID TO RUSSIA"

IN ENGLAND the various left wing parties who assist the war-for-democracy ideologists by misrepresenting Russia to the workers as a "workers' state", also offer varying policies. The Kremlin lackeys of the Communist Party are vociferating now (after a few initial hesitations) for maximum support for the Churchill Government. The Independent Labour Party on the other hand demands that Churchill and Co. must go, claiming that only a "workers' government" could or would give adequate support to Russia.

We might analyse these policies more deeply; but it is much more important to expose the false and mischievous assumption that underlies them all. That is, the idea that the workers of a class-divided nation can consciously and of themselves extend help to Russia.

Any assistance which goes out from this country is extended by the ruling group in this country, the workers, having no power, contribute only by falling in with its plans. Assistance afforded by a ruling class of any country to another country is intended to further the interests, not of the workers here or there, but of that ruling group itself. There is no altruism in international politics. Furthermore, any assistance which leaves this country, goes, not to the Russian workers, but to Stalin and Co., who will utilize it to suit their ends. All this should be obvious. If the workers wish to send help to the Russian workers they must first achieve their own emancipation here, and then assist the Russian workers to do the same in Russia. And neither of these aims has much to do with the imperialist war. Unless this is done, the whole idea of workers of one country assisting those of another is entirely worthless and misleading. The plain fact is that "assistance between nations" operates only for the mutual benefit of governments, not of workers at all (unless one believes that there is, or can be, a community of interests between exploiters and exploited). Intervention in Spain proved this, and the recent developments relating to the Sino-Japanese war, already referred to, is making it obvious.

We have discussed this question of "workers' aid to Russia" albeit briefly, because it is just one more of those pernicious illusions fostered by the left, which operate to prevent the workers from ever taking effective action to secure international solidarity with their class. It provides another instance of the invaluable assistance afforded by the left wing to the service of the right, in deflecting the attention of the working-class from its central task—the achievement of a classless society here. However much the workers may want to help their class brethren abroad, they must face the fact that it is simply impossible to do so while they are merely tools of the ruling class at home. That is why anarchists emphasize over and over again that class struggle provides the only means for the workers to achieve control over their destiny. To deflect them from this path only serves to foster illusions which continue to prevent the realization of effective, rather than merely wishful, international working-class solidarity. And the continual raising of false hopes can only lead to disillusionment and apathy.

August, 1941.

6. OUR NEW ALLY

WHEN A few months ago Hitler forced Russia to come into the war on our side the Republic of Soviets immediately lost its totalitarian character and became one of the great defenders of democracy. This metamorphosis must have caused some headaches to our journalists and politicians: the Russo-German pact was not so long ago nor were the Moscow trials. However, it did not take the Press more than a few weeks to endow Russia with all the attributes of a democratic country. All this whitewashing is superfluous as far as our new ally America is concerned. Their reputation of being a "great democracy" has never failed; not even when Tom Mooney was kept in prison nor when Sacco and Vanzetti were led to the electric chair. This belief is so deeply rooted in some people's minds that stories of negroes being lynched, of trade-unionists being beaten to death by the boss' hirelings, meet with incredulity. In spite of books and films describing the degrading life to which the negroes are submitted or the standard of starvation to which the unemployed and the evicted farmers are often reduced, America remains in the minds of the majority of people the land where workers go to work by car and where prejudices of all kinds are abolished.

The great democratic reputation enjoyed by America in Europe for more than a quarter of a century is entirely due to this "American Myth". It is obvious that neither President Wilson nor Roosevelt could have commanded such respect—not only amongst left-wing petit-bourgeois but also among the workers—if the truth about the nature of American democratic institutions had been known.

It is important to explode the myth; for too long the peoples of Europe have awaited the voice across the Atlantic to guide them in the right path. To what limits that voice will be allowed to guide us now depends on America's position in the war; her prestige and influence will increase in direct proportion to her victories in the Pacific and the output of her war industries.

Indifferent to that kind of consideration let us draw a balance sheet of America's fight for democracy at home up to the time of her entry into the war.

Like all countries fighting for democracy or preparing themselves to do so America has taken active steps to curtail the liberty of labour's organizations. Though no new anti-labour legislation was passed a serious blow was delivered at the right to strike by Mr. Roosevelt's method of sending the army to occupy factories where strikes were in process. The excuse was that "Our country is in danger". The greatest publicity was given to the strikes so as to create the impression that they paralysed the whole industry. In reality, according to Bruce Bliven in the Manchester Guardian "there have been fewer strikes in this period of sharply expanding industry and rising prices than ever before in the United States' history".

These strikes gave an excellent excuse to American capitalists to obtain anti-strike legislation. Democratic Isolationist deputies did not hesitate to resort to open blackmail in order to obtain these much coveted laws. When Roosevelt asked the House of Representatives to repeal the Neutrality Act, Democratic representatives threatened to oppose neutrality revision unless the Government put "a stop to labour dictatorships", thus making it clear that they were more anxious to crush labour unrest at home than to destroy the German navy in the Atlantic.

In order to pacify the democratic elements Roosevelt promised to consider anti-strike legislation. The newspapers announced at the time that he was considering an anti-strike programme to be modelled according to the plan in existence in Canada:

"Guarantee workers in the defence industries their present wage;
Guarantee them wage increases to meet any increased cost of living;
Demand from labour in return for these guarantees a pledge not to call further strikes in the defence industries."

The training of the army reflected also the anti-labour preoccupations of the ruling class. Instead of training the army to fight Japanese or German paratroops, recruits were trained in strike-breaking. Instruction in riot training was formerly restricted to state-controlled National Guard units. Recently training in strike-breaking, riot duty, street fighting and handling of mobs was extended to the regular army—which included the new conscripts.

George Seldes in the July 28th issue of In Fact gives examples of camps where anti-labour manœuvres are practised and quotes Press releases describing the training to which soldiers are being submitted. "It is a fact, he says, that instead of training boys to meet panzer divisions with tanks and guns, the first training received by many thousands of new soldiers is how to smash labour disputes, occupy mines, factories and towns", and he goes on to remark that these methods are the same ones that the private army of Benito Mussolini used in the 3-year period before he took power.

A proof that the administration will not hesitate to use the anti-democratic legislation it has taken into its hands under the Smith Act of 1940 is given by the indictment before a federal grand jury of 29 C.I.O. leaders and Socialist Workers' Party members on a charge of "seditious conspiracy". Previously to this anarchists had been prosecuted and prevented from publishing their newspaper, as in the case of Marcus Graham, editor of the long established anarchist paper *Man!* who has been imprisoned and prevented from resuming its publication.

Before its entry into the war the United States seemed to have gone further on the road to fascism than Great Britain after two years of war. Will the state of war accelerate this movement or not? It will all depend on the attitude adopted by the labour movement and on the success attending the conduct of the war.

We know already that as soon as Japan had declared war on America the Trade Union leaders called off the strikes in progress and pledged their full support for the successful prosecution of the war. As a result Roosevelt seems to have put aside for the time being his plans for anti-strike legislation. As in Britain therefore, the Trade Union leaders are prepared to sacrifice the interests of the workers. But war means rising prices and, in spite of their willingness to sacrifice the workers, Lewis and Green will be obliged to ask for a rise in wages. Just as Bevin and Co. here, they will have to meet the demands of the workers to a certain extent. Will American capitalists be willing to sacrifice part of their profits in order to prevent violent struggles which would weaken the war effort, or will they follow the road taken by the French ruling class who refused to even consider the workers' claims and a few hours after war was declared established a dictatorship which had nothing to learn from the Italian and German régimes?

The example of France has taught the ruling class that it is important that the façade of democracy should be preserved or the people lose all interest in the war and refuse to fight. The American Government will probably remember the lesson and will be careful to take away the workers' liberties one by one and with a great show of "mediation", and "arbitration", claiming to represent the opinion of the workers, the employers and public opinion alike but which, in reality, only serve the interests of the Government.

The American workers must not be fooled by these "democratic" methods. They must understand that as war difficulties increase, the democratic pretences of the Government will disappear and that they must defend their liberties and interests now before it is too late.

January, 1942.

7. DOWN WITH THE COLOUR BAR

THE ARRIVAL of American troops in this country has aroused the interest of the British people in the question of the colour bar. Many of them probably do not know that the colour bar exists in British Colonies and even if they do, have never given it any thought or considered it necessary to do something against it. Having to deal with coloured men they have to adopt an attitude towards the colour bar and it is interesting to note that in the majority of cases they refuse to apply any race discrimination. It was already noticeable in peace time that colour discrimination was greater amongst the 'upper class'. The colour bar was more frequent in smart restaurants in the West End than in working class districts. In towns like Newcastle, for example, coloured and white dockers drink together without any feeling of race discrimination.

The attitude of the population towards American troops confirms the peace time experience. In the villages and towns coloured troops have been received with sympathy by the people, shop-keepers often declaring that they prefer them to the white American troops because they are kinder and more polite, as shown by a letter to the *New Statesman* (29/8/42).

"Many of the townspeople, in fact, assert strongly that they
'prefer' the coloured troops to the white.   The effect of the 'segrega-
tion' on 'morale' is also interesting in some cases.   A typical remark
is 'it seems silly to talk about democracy when we have white
and black troops who will not talk or mix with one another'.   The
coloured soldiers are noted as being 'too reserved', 'careful', 'too self-
controlled and disciplined', and the construction put on these 'observations' is that the coloured have been 'cowed' by past inter-racial
experiences in the States.   In short, there is an obvious and fairly
definite tendency in many quarters towards championing the 'cause'
of the 'Blackies' (note the diminutive) against the white Americans.
The reaction of many of the latter is as might be expected.   They
appear to be at first very puzzled at events.   They cannot understand
that English attitude, more particularly the attitude of English women,
and are especially puzzled at the popularity of their coloured com-
patriots."

The sympathy and friendship shown towards coloured people,
is of course, worthy of every kind of encouragement and it would
have been easy to break down any prejudices which might still exist
by lectures, propaganda in the Press, entertainments which would have
brought whites and blacks together.   The policy of the Government
has been on the contrary to try to prevent the establishment of friendly
relations between coloured and white people.   At the request of the
military authorities such notices as the following have been put up
in pubs: "Coloured troops not served in this bar.   Entrance round
the corner".   Instructions have been issued to both male and female
British troops on the behaviour to adopt towards coloured troops.
"Critic" in the *New Statesman* writes that he knows "on fairly good
authority that the ruling in a certain area is that if an A.T.S. girl
is seen walking with a coloured soldier 'she should be removed to
another district, for another reason'."

A soldier wrote to the *Tribune* saying that a letter from the
Brigadier was read to them asking "that troops adopt an attitude
towards the Negro soldiers which was not unfriendly, but not 'too
friendly'."

"It was admitted that the average Englishman does not view
sympathetically the application of the colour bar in America, but that
this colour bar was accepted equally by both sides in the country of

its origin—in fact, the Negro soldiers themselves expected to find a similar system over here. In other words, the English troops need not fear that their natural friendliness towards visitors would be discredited were it toned down in the case of the Negroes.

The letter stated quite definitely, that Negro troops would not be allowed in the canteens, entertainments and dances organized for H.M. Forces. Members of the A.T.S. would be barred from public dances which were open to Negroes."

It is obvious that the military authorities would not take the trouble to make regulations preventing coloured and white troops mixing together and would not lecture soldiers on the necessity of adopting a not 'too friendly' attitude towards coloured troops, if hostility and prejudice against coloured people existed already. It is therefore surprising to see that the Minister of Information in an article on the colour bar (*Sunday Express* 20/9/42) attributes its existence in this country to the ignorance and insularity of the British people. He then goes on to declare, what is a patent hypocrisy,

" . . . that it is the desire of the British Government that this prejudice should go". "There is", he says, "no legal colour bar in this country, coloured people in Britain have in theory the same rights as any Englishman . . . but it is in fact true that there is still some colour prejudice in this country and still social barriers against coloured people . . . I should like to say at once that the British Government is in favour of putting an end to this prejudice as quickly as possible.

"We in Britain are determined to see that the victory for which we are striving will be as much theirs (the black people of the colonial empire) as ours. The barriers still standing in the way of the social equality of the coloured people must be withdrawn. The prejudiced must be taught by precept and example, to overcome their prejudices. This is a process which will take time, but responsible people in Britain are determined that it shall be carried through, and the sooner the better."

What is there behind these high sounding declarations? Far from wanting to put an end to the colour bar, the British Government accepts it in the colonies and encourages it in this country. Has not the Government always closed its eyes to the scandalous attitude

of West End hotels which have refused to accept coloured customers?
If the Government really wanted to abolish the colour bar, how does
Mr. Brenden Bracken explain that the colour bar exists in British
colonies? It is illogical to expect civil servants who have lived all
their lives in the colonies, where the colour bar is considered as one
of the pillars of the British Empire, to come back to this country
and behave towards coloured people as if they were their equals.

Now the Government has a splendid opportunity to show the
wonderful lack of prejudice with which it is blessed—according to
our Minister of Information. It could show its lack of prejudice
towards American coloured troops, but on the contrary, it adopts
a Blimpish attitude and is only too pleased to lick the boots of the
American authorities who, not content with having the colour bar
in their own country, want the British people to respect their backward reactionary attitude towards coloured people.

The attitude adopted by the British Government towards American troops demonstrates once more that any progress made against
race discrimination will be made in spite of the Government. The
Colour Bar is just one aspect of the Government's policy of divide
and rule. Just as it is in the interests of Hitler to play off the
Gentiles against the Jews so is it in the interest of the British Government to maintain or create a division between white and coloured
people.

American troops are coming to this country in order to bring
"freedom and democracy" to the people of Europe. If we are not
careful not only will they not liberate Europe but they will help to
establish a reactionary régime in this country. British people cannot
do very much at present to abolish race prejudice on the continent
but they can do a lot to eradicate it from this country and from the
American troops over here. Instead of deploring, as certain people
have done, that so many coloured people should have been sent over
here, they should welcome this opportunity to put into practice the
true principles of fraternity between races without which wars cannot
be abolished. Though Americans may at first be puzzled and even
shocked by the absence of prejudice towards coloured people, they
cannot but be impressed by it, and when they go back to America,
they may help to get rid of the colour bar in their own country.

October, 1942.

8. THE AMERICAN ELECTIONS

THE FARCE of democracy goes on. To maintain the illusion of government representing the will of the people, there is no trouble or expense to which the ruling class in the so-called democratic countries would not go. The Americans are particularly extravagant in staging the democratic show. The presidential elections last year absorbed a tremendous amount of the country's energies and money. To enable the American people to choose its president, financiers and capitalists poured money into the propaganda funds of Roosevelt and Willkie. When the money was spent, the invectives exchanged, and the President elected, the American people were informed that there was no real difference between the programme of the two candidates, that the insults exchanged were merely for propaganda purposes and that the two rivals were now going to work together in close collaboration.

Now the American people have had the privilege of electing the House of Representatives and a third of the Senate in the biennial elections. Unlike the British Government, the American has not considered it necessary to suppress elections during the war, though the people know that particularly in war time the power resides in the hands of the President who can over-rule Congress when he chooses. Nobody seemed to enjoy the comedy of the elections; "everybody will be heartily glad when they are over" writes the *Manchester Guardian,* and American journals declared before the elections that both the public and the Press had no faith in Congress. According to the New York *Times,* the people of the U.S. no longer look to Congress for leadership, for advice, even for debates or oratory; "they watch Congress mainly for laughs". This doesn't mean of course that American journalists and politicians would gladly see the end of the parliamentary racket; such conclusions would upset a system in which they flourish, and they limit themselves to asking the people to elect better representatives and at the same time want a stronger leadership—that is to say more power in the hands of the President.

One of the reasons for the unpopularity of Congress is that it has given many proofs that it is concerned with protecting its own interests or those of the various capitalist groups it represents—sometimes in the most reckless way. Congress aroused a great deal of indignation at the time of Pearl Harbour when it voted the Congressional Retirement Plan, of Jan. 21, 1942.

"American soldiers were dying in the grim siege of Bataan and Singapore was soon to fall. The nation was awaiting the truth about Pearl Harbour from the Roberts report, issued Jan. 23. The people were heartsick and badly hurt. And then they read in their newspapers that Congress had voted itself pensions out of the public treasury.

That was just too much. The whole country exploded with righteous anger. In Spokane thousands of voters joined in a freakish 'Bundles for Congress' campaign, contributing old dental plates, wooden legs and razor blades for 'the relief of indigent Congressmen'. The New York *Times* called the bill an illustration 'of Congress' apparent complacency and willingness to put self-interest above the nations interest'. President Roosevelt signed the bill on Jan. 24, but Congress got it back and repealed it in a hurry." *Life* 17/9/42.

The Senate puts its own interests before those of the nation in the same shameless way. The *Manchester Guardian* (3/11/42) reported that the production of war equipment is hampered because the 'silver senators' will not release the Government from commitments undertaken in 1934 and thus allow it to use silver reserves for industrial purposes. This is how democracy worked in this particular case:

"In 1934 the twelve senators from the six chief silver mining States made an alliance with the Farm Block on the understanding that they would vote for each other's bills. One of the results was the Silver Purchase Act, which not only obliged the Treasury to purchase both foreign and domestic silver, but provided that the Treasury cannot sell any silver at less than $1.29 an ounce, which is nearly three times the world market price and nearly twice the price fixed for domestic silver purchases. Since then, the Treasury has accumulated a great hoard of silver which is now buried in a vault at West Point, New York." The Treasury is forbidden to sell its silver for industrial purposes by the twelve 'silver senators'. After long negotiations they allowed the lending of some Treasury silver to American industry, provided it was used only for strictly defined purposes to make sure it would all be returned after the war. The only use so far found within these restrictions, described here recently, is in 'bus bars', electric conductors."

Congress may seem sometimes to be concerned with the interests of sections of the population but the reason behind it is the desire to acquire popularity. This is more important for Congressmen than for M.P.'s in this country as they have to be re-elected every two years.

"Congress played politics with the soldier's pay bill, when it raised the base pay for privates from $21 a month to $50, instead of the $42 which the Army and Navy had asked for. A few extra dollars, thought Congressmen, might give them a few extra votes. Congress is playing politics every hour on rubber, on gasoline, on all the petty little local woes of the nation. The pages of the *Congressional Record* are crammed with appeals for special consideration for the motorists of the East, for the motorists of the South, for the motorists of the Midwest and of the Pacific Coast. Senators and Representatives have shed oceans of printed tears over oil producers and oil shippers and oil distributors and would-be oil buyers. A future historian might conclude that all the U.S. had to think about in the summer of 1942 was how to burn up its oil and gasoline on the home front." *Life* 17/9/42.

The fact that there is one representative for every 301,164 people in the United States is enough to make one dizzy with the stupidity of the system. It is absolutely impossible for a man to represent the wishes and defend the interests of three hundred thousand people.

Of the 432 Representatives in Congress, 251 are lawyers, 32 business men, 18 farmers, 17 publishers and journalists, 15 educators, 12 insurance men and nine bankers. In a highly industrialised country there is not a single industrial worker in Congress! But it is the workers who mainly provide the money for this expensive show; it is they who work to provide Congressmen with a salary of £2,500 a year. Do they really believe that the expense is worth while? The fact that at the recent election only 15,000,000 out of an electorate of 42 millions voted, seems to show that people do not really feel they can achieve anything through elections. It shows that people are aware that the government is the instrument of the ruling class

and that it is therefore useless for them to pretend to take part in it.
And yet, according to the American constitution, an Anarchist, *i.e.* a
person who does not believe in any form of government, cannot become
an American citizen!

November, 1942.

9. THE BURMA EVACUATION

WHEN THE British evacuated Burma the Indian Nationalist leaders
accused the Europeans of having received preferential treatment. The
Europeans they said, were able to leave Burma along the so-called
"white route" which was much shorter than the "black route" which
the Indians were obliged to take. This was a serious accusation and
one would have expected the Press to shed some light on the truthful-
ness of it. The fact that the conditions of the Burmese evacuation
were ignored by most newspapers seems to indicate that the divulging
of facts would not be to the credit of the white sahibs in Burma.

The *News Chronicle* carried an account of the evacuation which
seemed to confirm that the Europeans did receive preferential treatment. War Correspondent, William Munday, in a cable to his newspaper (29/7/42) begins by stating that those in charge of the evacuation refute the claim of the Indian Nationalist leaders that the
Europeans had preferential treatment but the facts he goes on to
relate, contradict this statement. He first of all admits that the
Indians did not choose the "black route" through the mountains,
since he says: "They (the Indian evacuees) were diverted also so
that Indians working on one of these roads (the "white road") would
not be upset by the sufferings of their fellow countrymen and women".
Who can believe that the Indians were diverted from the "white road"
for such a reason? Since when are our officials in the Empire so
anxious to spare the feelings of the natives? And we can imagine
how the Indians working on the "white road" appreciated the sight
of the well fed Europeans rushing to safety when they probably
knew of their countrymen dying of cold and hunger along the inter-
minable "black road".

The *News Chronicle* correspondent justifies the preferential treatment received by the whites with the argument that as the Indians were more numerous than the Europeans they could not have all gone by the white route. He does not think it necessary to explain why the Europeans were saved rather than some of the Indians!

"The Indians came over the so-called "black route", which is much longer but much easier than the other routes and along which there was no limit on numbers. More than 200,000 used it from February to June, many getting free rides in carts and motor vehicles.

The white routes meant a trip along the river or over many hilly miles. The first was limited by the number of boats available and only 60 to 80 were brought in that way every three days. The second was limited by the number of elephants available and its capacity was 60 persons daily."

Thanks to the boats and the elephants, the Europeans arrived safely in India, while the Indians struggled along the black road dying by the thousand.

"During the next month, however, 25,000 Indians, including unexpected refugees, streamed into India. They were in a pitiful condition, and officially 20 per cent. of them died of exhaustion, malnutrition, dysentery, cholera or malaria on the 20-day journey from the Indo-Burma frontier."

According to the *News Chronicle* correspondent, one of the causes of the difficulties of the evacuation was "the generally poor physique and stamina of the refugees". The unfortunate inhabitants of the British Empire work like beasts of burden for starvation wages in peace time, and when it suits us to wage a "war for democracy" we let them die of exhaustion, dysentery or cholera.

September, 1942.

10. HELL SHIPS FOR REFUGEES

THE NEWSPAPERS are filled with stories of Nazi atrocities in occupied Europe; journalists and editors shed tears over the martyrs of Hitler's régime, and politicians swear that help and revenge will come. One would therefore think that when Vichy France allows Polish, Austrian, Italian, Russian and French refugees to leave the European inferno they would be received in the democratic countries with open arms and be given all possible facilities to live and work. Nothing of the kind, however, happens; European refugees are not allowed even to land in the "democratic" states of South America. The following report taken from *L'Adunata**, quotes *Time* (1/12/41) to show how the inhuman methods of the Vichy Government have been more than equalled by those of the "friends of democracy" in South America.

"A year ago, a group of Jewish refugees, coming from Poland, Austria, Czechoslovakia, France, Italy, Switzerland, and even Russia, had secured permission from the Vichy Government to embark on the ship "Alsina" bound for Brazil. Each refugee had been accorded a special visa for that country. The "Alsina" was about to sail from Dakar, when an order came from Vichy preventing it from leaving the port. For four and a half months the "Alsina" remained anchored at Dakar with her human cargo.

The ship was then transferred to Casablanca in French Morocco. The refugees were interned in a concentration camp where several died. Towards the end of the summer, 40 were allowed to embark on the "Cabo de Buena Esperanza" where the conditions were even worse than on the "Alsina": the ship was overcrowded, filthy, infected, stinking; the food uneatable. In the sick berths old newspapers were used instead of sheets. During the journey two refugees died.

Arriving at Rio de Janeiro they were prevented from landing on the pretext that the visa obtained at Dakar was valid only for 90 days and this period had long since expired.

A few days afterwards the "Cabo de Buena Esperanza" resumed her journey towards Argentine. There the refugees obtained permission to stop for 90 days in the 'Immigrants' House' during which period they were ordered to secure a refuge. Before the end of the 90 days Ramon Castillo (President of Argentine) gave the order for them to leave. All of them had secured a permit to enter Paraguay but Castillo refused to give them a permit to cross the city in order

*The Italian anarchist weekly published in the United States.

to embark in the ship which would have brought them to Paraguay. They were instead crowded on the "Cabo de Hornos" where there were already 57 refugees from the original group of the "Alsina".

Before the "Cabo" weighed anchor one of her passengers committed suicide. At Rio de Janeiro two refugees were able to land. Despair reigned on board. The Captain frankly told the journalists that his passengers would have committed suicide *en masse* rather than return to Europe. For the whole night the port police surrounded the boat in order to pick up those who would have committed suicide.

But the Brazilian authorities did not change their mind, and the tragic ship resumed her journey.

At the end of November the Dutch government allowed the refugees of the "Cabo de Hornos" to land temporarily at Willemstadt, capital of the Island of Curacao in the East Indies.

The number of the refugees who landed was 79."

How long will the workers allow their governments to act in such an inhuman way towards refugees? After the Spanish war hundreds of thousands of refugees were left shelterless and hungry on French territory. They were treated like animals and many were handed over to Franco. No movements of protest, no strikes took place in order to demonstrate the solidarity of the French and British workers towards the victims of Franco. Now the American workers show the same indifference towards those who, after tremendous hardships, have succeeded in leaving Europe. We know that governments, even if they call themselves democratic, are not concerned with the lives of persecuted men and women. The example quoted above is but one of many cases which have occurred in the last few years. We have seen letters from Spanish refugees in Mexico who found the conditions there so appalling that they wanted to return to Europe; we know of cases of old Italian anti-fascists who preferred Mussolini's jails to Daladier's concentration camps. Democratic governments will allow hospitality and comfortable homes to the Queen Geraldines, Jugo-Slav princelings and Dutch princesses but it is for the workers to see that their refugee brothers are not left to starve and die on hell ships or in concentration camps.

February, 1942.

11. QUISLINGITIS

"I am happy to express in the name of our commander-in-chief as well as in my own the pleasure that we have had in concluding the agreement that has been made known to you with Admiral Darlan and the French military authorities."—Lt.-General Clark, Deputy C-in-C Allied Forces, North Africa, broadcast from Morocco radio."   *Manchester Guardian,* 17/11/42.

"Only a revolutionary Britain could offer such assistance to working-class Europe. Which country it will be that makes its revolution first and offers such assistance to the world revolution remains to be seen. One thing is certain, the defeat of Hitler by revolutionary means could not be done by capitalist Britain."
War Commentary, Sept., 1941.

WHEN THE Americans landed in North Africa, President Roosevelt sent a message to the French people declaring "again and again" his "faith in liberty, equality and fraternity" and promising "that the Americans with the help of the United Nations are doing all they can to establish a healthy future as well as the restoration of the ideal of freedom and democracy for all those who have lived under the Tricolour". This declaration was followed by an alliance with the French Quisling, Darlan. Americans had taken a leaf from the Nazi experience of invasion, and they used all the crooks they could find and invited them into the allied camp to avoid fighting them. The healthy future for liberty, fraternity and equality, promised by President Roosevelt turned out to be liberty for the fascist politicians, equality for the Darlans who were treated with all the "consideration due to their rank", fraternity with Laval's acolytes of yesterday. A reactionary like Giraud took undisputed command of the French forces, and Darlan, the super-Quisling was nominated chief of the Government, and included in his Government the fascist, Flandin, and the Cagoulard and member of Doriot's Party, Pucheux. No doubt, if Laval himself had happened to be in North Africa at the time there would have been no rank high enough to give him.

The Darlan Affair has caused a lot of surprise and indignation in the Allied camp since so many people look upon Roosevelt as a second Washington. In reality this is nothing more than an incident

in the relations between democratic and fascist countries and fits
in well with the others. The American government maintained
friendly relations with the French government up to the last moment.
The United States ambassador Admiral Leahy was in friendly relations with Pétain while manifesting hostility to the Free French
Movement. Britain does not lag behind in making advances to
fascist rulers. Sir Samuel Hoare is reported to be on the best terms
with Franco, there is now also a tendency in this country to represent
Franco as an unwilling tool in Hitler's hands and it is rumoured that
Sir Samuel would be only too glad to put his name to a Franco-Hoare
pact which would guarantee Franco's régime and perhaps enlarge
its possessions. If the Christian gentleman who bled Spain for three
years and who is responsible for the death, imprisonment and starvation of millions of Spaniards may become a friend and his Spain
hailed by Churchill as "free and independent", what is wrong with
Darlan being one too?

The only person who should feel cheated is poor General de
Gaulle! To be hailed as the Saviour of France for two years and
then to be let down in favour of people who have condemned him
and his friends to death, (and who have shot a few when possible)
is hard luck. Gangsters are reputed to honour their pledges; the
General must wish politicians did.

Left Wing papers have not General de Gaulle's excuse for
feeling surprise and indignation. They should know better than
to believe that Roosevelt and Churchill were going to put themselves
at the head of the French People to bring about their liberation.
The jailers of the Indian people and the complacent spectators of
negro pogroms are hardly fitted for the rôle of leaders of *sans-culotte*.

Left Wing newspapers' protests are pathetic. Journalists seem
to have been taken in by their own lies. Take the *Tribune*:

"Parliament and the people have the immediate task of repudiat-
ing the action of generals and diplomats in flat contradiction to the
principle for which we have gone to war. Thousands have gone to
their deaths that this shall not happen. It must not happen."

This sounds very stirring, but it should be obvious to the *Tribune*

WAR COMMENTARY

For Anarchism

Vol. 4 No. 21.   SEPTEMBER 1943.   TWOPENCE

BRITISH BOMBING has brought death to many thousands of people in the past few weeks. At Quebec, politicians who provide themselves with shelters well out of reach of bombs, are planning to continue massive bombing as a means of carrying on the "war against fascism".

Hamburg, Milan, Genoa, Turin, are covered with ruins, their streets heaped with bodies and streaming with blood. "Hamburgizing" is coming into use as a new term for wholesale destruction of cities, and the mass murder of their populations through terrorist raids. The Press boasts of the R.A.F.'s power to carry such destruction to all the cities of Germany and Central Europe. It screamed with indignation when the Germans bombed churches and hospitals, but now it gloats over the destruction of entire cities ... "In Hamburg there are not fifty houses left untouched by our bombing raids". The Press wept crocodile tears over chained prisoners of war, but when the smell of carnage goes up from once beautiful and populous towns they find words of rejoicing. When the water mains broke in Milan, and flooded the centre of the city, they find it a subject for a joke. "Lake Milan" the clever journalist calls it. What does it matter to him if "the water is flowing between the ruins and the debris of bombed buildings, and people living in the district were forced to remain in the wreckage of their homes for four days until the water

ii. The Folly of Bombing
March 1944

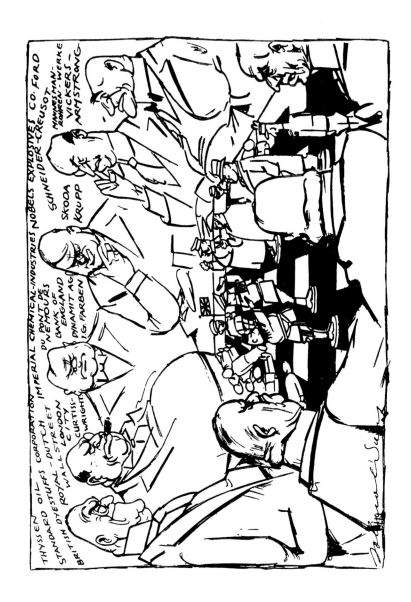

iii. No title
March 1943

iv. Beveridge Pie in the Sky
mid-January 1943

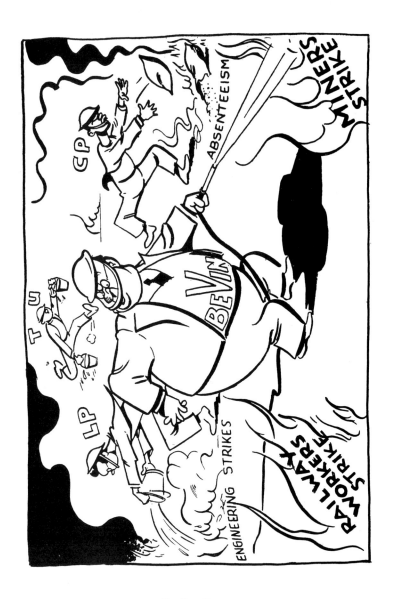

v. Strikes Increase
mid-April 1943

vi. No title
May 1943

vii. Why don't the Italian People Revolt?
July 1943

viii. Day of Prayer

that capitalists, politicians, generals and diplomats have gone to war for reasons of their own, and what they have given the people to believe is not going in any way to determine their attitude ... They have gone to war to defend the British Empire, 'to hold our own' as Churchill put it: they have gone to war to defend Christianity, that is to say the principles upheld by Franco and Co.; they have gone to war to reinforce their position and this cannot be done if France is free; to have revolution just across the Channel is obviously not an advantage for the ruling class here. What France needs is a strong government, which will keep the French people in order, and leaders who don't object to taking their orders from London or Washington.

Churchill and Roosevelt are right from their capitalist and imperialist point of view. It is the left-wing journalists who expect a reactionary government to act in a liberal way, to sanction revolts, who are illogical. Neither the British nor the American or Russian governments are prepared to give power to the people. They know that agreements can always be reached with the Darlans and the Francos, but that when the people revolt they may overthrow all rulers, fascist and "democratic" alike.

If the allies' victories continue, many more fascist rats will leave the Axis' sinking ship, and be welcomed to the democratic camp. And that is as it should be. The rats who helped Mussolini to conquer Abyssinia, who helped Franco to crush the Spanish revolution, who armed Japan against China, who bombed the Arabs and the Indians, come together when it suits them. The people of France will realise that the friends of Darlan will never help them to crush fascism; the Spanish workers will understand that if Britain supports Franco it cannot defend freedom.

Everywhere workers will understand that it is not through military or diplomatic victories that Fascism will be crushed. Only an alliance of the workers of all countries against their oppressors and exploiters can end fascism.

December, 1942.

12. FASCISTS AT WORK IN ALGERIA

THE LATEST political moves in North Africa have been greeted with
something approaching delight by certain sections of the English
'Left', and their Press, from the *Manchester Guardian* to the *Daily
Worker,* has praised the new set-up resulting from the latest reshuffle
of reactionary bigwigs. The *Daily Worker* (8/2/43) describes the
development as a 'blow to Vichy men', and remarks that "under the
pressure of public opinion, Giraud has been enabled to make considerable headway against the Vichyites, but the Vichyites have by
no means as yet exhausted their ammunition or their power to prevent
a much bigger extension of unity under the banner of Fighting
French." A significant characteristic of their commentary is the way
in which the Communists are trying to present Giraud as an angelic
liberal struggling against the reactionary tendencies of his associates,
whom even the *Daily Worker* cannot claim as enthusiastic anti-Fascists.
The *Manchester Guardian* (8/2/43) appears to share this illusion of
Giraud as the gallant democrat, for in its editorial remarks it says
"General Giraud has taken further measures to give broader authority
to his Administration and a more liberal character to his policy".

Let us examine the measures taken by General Giraud, in an
attempt to discover the liberalism on which his admirers are so
emphatic, and also to elucidate the manner in which democratic principles are applied in the liberation of countries formerly subjected
to Fascist tyranny.

To begin, let us admire the democratic way in which General
Giraud reached his position. In fact, he was elected to it by himself
and the few associates who formed Darlan's Imperial Council and
now form Giraud's War Committee. These associates, Peyrouton,
Boisson, and Generals Nogues and Bergeret, are all supporters of
Vichy and admirers, avowed or otherwise, of Fascist methods, which
they have been applying in Africa for the last two years since the fall
of France. Giraud, having been elected by the Imperial Council
to the position of Civil and Military Commander-in-Chief, issued a
proclamation saying that he had "assumed" this position and that
the new War Committee would consist of Governors and "other
persons who are being or might be invited by General Giraud."

This assumption of power was not preceded even by the pretence of an accord between the various French parties and movements. General de Gaulle was not consulted, and the appointments do not appear to have been discussed even during the much-publicised conversation between Churchill, Roosevelt, de Gaulle and Giraud.

General Giraud also invested himself with the right to name governors, magistrates, university heads, etc. He has, moreover, the right to dispose of the 'legal and political status of any person', whether French or foreign, in Algeria. If this is democracy, then one wonders why Hitler should put his democrats in concentration camps. But perhaps the democrats in the concentration camps of North Africa think a little differently!

It is estimated that these concentration camps hold at least 65,000 people in some seventeen camps, eight in Algeria and nine in Morocco. It is further believed that a number of new camps have been established, and that since the arrival of the liberators in North Africa a number of new prisoners of revolutionary or de Gaullist sympathies have been added to those already incarcerated. The new measures have included the release of some of these internees, but it is significant to see how the released men have been chosen.

After the Communist deputy Grenier had pledged the official support of the Communist Party to the War Committee, some 27 Communist deputies who had been kept in prison in Algiers for more than two years were released. The propaganda value of this move is obvious, and it is further significant that there has been no general release of rank-and-file Communists or of revolutionaries or democrats.

Men of military age and fitness are to be released, whether they are Fascists or not. In this connection Giraud remarked: 'When I see a member of the S.O.L. (a French Fascist organisation) and I hear that he is imprisoned, I look at his record. I may find he is a good fighter. I release him.' Men not fit for military service, on the other hand, whether they are democrats or not, must await an investigation commission of mixed French and American representatives. The commission, however, has no power to release them. This can only be done by the French authorities, and as these are mostly Vichy men it will be seen how much this provision is worth.

Almost all the members of the War Committee have shown anti-semitic tendencies in the past, and Peyrouton was the originator of a number of laws against the Jews in Vichy France, and one of the prime instigator of the persecution of French Jews. It is therefore not surprising that Giraud should have announced that he was going to solve the Jewish problem gradually, and not 'by a stroke of a pen or a stroke of a sword'. The Jews have been given back their property, and Jewish children can attend schools, while a limited number of Jews are to be admitted to the professions. The Jews, however, are still deprived of their political rights, in spite of the fact that since 1871 all inhabitants of North Africa have been regarded as having equal rights to those of French citizens.

The right of association has not been restored, so that workers, whether French or native, are not allowed to revive their trade unions or syndicates. A number of syndicalists who took advantage of their liberation in this way have been placed in concentration camps.

From these facts it would appear that the measures taken by General Giraud are intended purely as propaganda to nourish the illusion in England and America that the new French régime in North Africa is really democratic. In fact, it remains a dictatorial régime whose Fascist characteristics have been mitigated only to the least degree required for the purposes of deception.

The Nazis are now celebrating the tenth anniversary of their seizure of power in Germany. In that acquisition of power they were assisted materially by the reactionary interests of England and America. Later, when German aeroplanes and tanks were destroying the Spanish Revolution, they were again assisted by British and American conservative interests, while the representatives of the British government outclassed Pontius Pilate at the washing of hands. Now, after Britain has been nominally at war with Fascism for more than three years and America for two years, we find the same people aiding and abetting the perpetuation of Fascist government, under men like Peyrouton with recent records of close collaboration with Hitler, in the very countries to which their troops are supposed to have come as liberators. This was shown very clearly in the House of Commons on the 4th February, when Eden defended the Anglo-American position by saying that:

"Both Governments wished to see that traditional freedom which flourished on French soil once more re-established both in North

Africa and in France itself, and for this reason both were agreed that nothing must be allowed to distract them from the first and imperative duty of developing the maximum military effort upon which all depended."

The old story of pie in the sky!

February, 1943.

13. WAR AND FASCISM

IN THE years before the war, the British working class often expressed its hatred of Fascism. The spontaneous erection of barricades in the streets of the East End to frustrate Mosley's marches were an example. Workers hated Hitler for the brutality of Nazi concentration camps and the vicious anti-semitism. They hated Mussolini for the Abyssinian war. During those pre-war years when our ruling class was friendly towards the Fascist powers and coldly sacrificed the smaller states, as they successively fell victims to Fascist aggression, the workers were solidly anti-fascist.

Unlike Sir John Simon and Mr. Amery, the English people have been particularly sympathetic towards the Chinese in their fight against Japan. And the fact that Britain and America at long last formed an alliance with China did much to strengthen the propaganda of the ruling class about the anti-fascist war for freedom. But sympathy for the Chinese struggle, like the sympathy with the Russians, has made people idealize the Chinese Generalissimo, Chiang Kai-Shek as a front-line fighter for freedom.

The *Observer* (10/10/43) is nearer the truth, however, when it describes China as "no more than a self-constituted dictatorship under the Kuomintang", and Chiang Kai-Shek as "frankly a military dictator."

But now that China is in the news, more information is forthcoming which is likely to undermine idealistic hopes about the Sino-Japanese war. Thus the source quoted above reveals that China has now been fully opened up as a field for imperialist investment:

"Immediately after Chiang's election (as President), and in response to a powerful speech made by him last month, the Central Executive Committee (the highest governing body) lifted all restrictions hitherto applying to Sino-foreign enterprise in China. Henceforward the bulk of the capital need not be Chinese, the general manager may be a foreigner, and foreigners may be permitted to finance their own enterprises in China."

In England it is an offence to trade with the enemy. It is therefor doubly disillusioning to find that the Chinese Government still trades with the territory occupied by Japan! The *Manchester Guardian* (19/11/43) correspondent in Chungking states that:

"Trade between Japanese-occupied and Free China has recently taken on larger proportions on account of the Chinese Government's endeavour to attract useful goods from enemy territory . . . Value of the known imports from occupied areas to Free China during the last six months, according to a Government spokesman, was £1,250,000 sterling on Government account, and £25,000,000 through commercial channels.

China's struggle "for freedom" is carried on under a "frank military dictatorship"; and while millions of Chinese workers have died fighting the Japanese, the Government and the Chinese capitalists do business with the other side to the tune of more than £26,000,000 a half year.

Hatred of Hitler and the desire to join with Spain and China in the fight against Fascist Aggression, provided the British Government with the support it required when, four and a half years ago, they entered the Second Imperialist War. In 1939 it was to avenge and defend freedom and small nations that we took up arms. But things are changed since then! Now even the blah-blah propagandists mix their "ideals" with a strong materialistic flavour. Here is the American paper, *Life*:

"America is the symbol of freedom . . . and all over the world now, there are living fragments of this symbol, and all over the world they are being shot down . . . When these living units of freedom are extinguished we cannot bring them back to life. All we can do is to give meaning to their death.

"And this is to say that when freedom falls, as it has here on the beach at Buna, it is our task to cause it to rise again; not in living units, which we cannot make and to which we cannot give life, but in the mighty symbol, America, the beacon for all men, which is ours to have, to hold, and to increase."

Yet for all its absurdity, this patriotic blurb does attempt to give idealism and meaning to the sacrifice of life which the war involves. But statesmen are becoming increasingly blunt, virtually declaring the "war for freedom" to be a war of conquest. Smuts in his recent speech stated that there would only be three great powers after the war—the British Empire, the United States and Russia. Harry Hopkins, Lease-Lend Administrator and close friend of Roosevelt is even more frank in an article quoted in the *Daily Mirror* on December 3rd:

"We will emerge from this war the richest and most powerful people in the world. Make no mistake about it. When the 'cease fire' is finally sounded we alone of all the Great Powers will find our lands unbombed and unscarred; our people well nourished and strong; and our breadbasket still filled to overflowing.

"We will have the largest navy and merchant fleet in the seven seas, more aeroplanes than any other nation."

We have certainly travelled a long way since the 1939 protestations about "no territorial aggrandisement", about preventing one nation (Germany) seeking hegemony in Europe or even world domination.

Fascism stands for the exaltation of the leadership principle, for the placing of the destiny of a whole people in the hands of one man, the leader. It was to destroy this spirit that the people of England fell in behind Chamberlain in 1939. Yet reporting the recent conferences of the "Big Three", such headlines as "These men shape the future of the world" have been common.

The change in war propaganda reflects the increasing control of the State over the individual lives of men and women (yet another attribute of Fascism) which war legislation has accomplished. Perhaps the clearest reflexion of the drift towards totalitarian and authoritarian conceptions is to be seen in the many plans for post-war reconstruction. The Beveridge Plan and its revised and amended versions as well as all the other propositions put forward to solve the post-war problems, are united in this: that they all envisage extended control by the State over everything that concerns the lives of men and women and even children, from questions of unemployment to questions of charity. Military and industrial conscription, and compulsory semi-military youth organisations to absorb the leisure of the young, are all put forward and extolled, not as the attributes of a Fascism they really represent, but as benefits conferred by wise leaders of a benevolent State. Freedom becomes ever and increasingly an abstract conception, with a smaller and smaller place in the life of to-day, and still less, apparently, of to-morrow.

Thus as the war drags on—already it has lasted longer than the war of 1914-18—it uncovers more unworthy and discreditable motives, while the tendency becomes ever more clearly to enthrone that form of authoritarian rule which it is alleged to be fighting against. Many who hoped (and some who fought against Franco in Spain are amongst them) to see the war against Hitler become in real earnest a war against Fascist reaction have become disillusioned. Events have proved that wars for freedom cannot be waged by the class enemies of freedom. Instead the principle of obedience to authority has been enormously strengthened.

In the Anarchists' manifesto on war* we have opposed the war because it is *not* a war for Freedom, because it has always been a war of conquest, a war for imperialist gain. We do not point only to theoretical considerations however to support our position. Events are the most cogent teachers of all. It is the logic of events that will bring the workers of the world in disgust to throw down the institutions of power and government whose rivalry has for the second time in thirty years soaked the whole world in blood. Events will bring them to join hands across the frontiers in the Social Revolutionary fight against Fascism, and the reconstruction not of the old, evil, cruel world of Capitalism, but of the free association of free men holding their destinies in their own hands.

December, 1943.

*Published in *War Commentary* Mid-Dec., 1943—ED.

14. STATE CONTROL OR WORKERS CONTROL

MANY OF those pro-war-for-democracy-and-socialism people now realise that, this war, far from abolishing privileges and inequalities, is putting an increased burden on the shoulders of the working class. Up to now the working class has had to suffer from the loss of its political rights, and on the material side from an increase in the cost of living, rationing, longer working hours, etc., Mr. Bevin's new decree adds further restrictions to the liberty and welfare of the workers. Labour in "scheduled establishments" is to be conscripted. A worker will no longer be able to choose the job he likes or to leave a place where he does not earn enough or where he has been submitted to some injustice by the boss or foreman. He will not be able to leave his job without the permission of the National Service Officer. Furthermore he can be ordered to take an unwanted job as well as prevented from leaving it. The Defence Regulations provide penalties for those who refuse to comply with the orders received.

To give the decree a certain flavour of impartiality the following rules which have the appearance of restricting the liberty of the employer have been laid down.

The employer will not be allowed to dismiss a worker except for "serious misconduct". Now that labour, especially in war industries is scarce, it is obvious that it is in the interests of the employer not to dismiss a worker for a trifle anyway.

The workman will receive a guaranteed weekly wage in accordance with the time wages recognised in the trade, or in collective agreements. This sounds better than it is in reality as in many factories the wages are nowadays higher than those recognised by the Trades Unions. Furthermore, with the rapid increase in the cost of living there is no agreement or contract which can be of any value for any length of time.

Tribunals with representatives of the employers and the workers with an impartial chairman will advise the National Service officers. Considering the results of other Tribunals (Conscientious Objectors' for example) run on similar lines one may safely predict that they will be a farce like the others and that there will be no need to modify the old saying that "might is right".

Now, what do our pro-war-for-democracy-and-socialism partisans advocate against this unjust suppression of the workers' liberties?

Nothing against conscription of labour itself.   They think it necessary
but they demand equality of sacrifice.   And they expect the State
to impose that equality.   They would like it to take over essential
war industries so as to impose some sacrifices on the capitalists.   *The
New Statesman and Nation* (1/3/41) suggests that:

"If the workman is to be forced to serve in a particular factory,
whether he likes it or not, and whether or not he could better his
economic position by going elsewhere, the factory in which he is to
serve must belong to the State.   To compel him to serve the private
capitalist is—Nazism and nothing else."

How will the State take over war industries?   Will it just deprive
the capitalists of their property or pay them compensation?   In the
latter case it is the workers who will have to make the sacrifices in
order to pay that compensation.   To what extent this will improve
their morale we don't know.

To imagine that the State is going to establish equality of sacrifice is to assume that the State is impartial, that it has no interest in
favouring one class rather than another.   But who forms the State?
Who controls it?   Who is employed in it if not the representatives
of the capitalist class, the aristocracy and the bourgeoisie?   When
people like Mr. Bevin are allowed to join the government it is because
they have abandoned all that made them the representatives of the
working class (their actions in the government well prove it).

In this country "big business" still reigns and the State is an
embodiment of it.   No political party, no Trade Union organisation
has been strong enough to master the State and succeed in controlling
the capitalists.   This does not mean that Big Business will not have
to put itself on rations.   It may have to do so if it sees (or is sufficiently alive to its own interests to see) that there is no other way of
emerging from the war still on top.   It will not be done from an
altruistic desire to establish equality of sacrifice but because there
will be no other way out.

The same article in the *New Statesman and Nation* refers to the
closing down by the Board of Trade, of a large number of factories
which do not produce essential commodities for the war.   Thus we
assume that the factory owners will be compensated for the losses
they may have incurred in the closing down or transformation of

their factories.   This may be the beginning of the restrictive measures that the capitalists have to impose on themselves.   But could this be called a socialist measure?   Not at all.   The factories which will be closed will, most of them, be factories whose trade was declining because of the war restrictions.   The owners of big armament factories remain in their privileged situation.   In the capitalist class itself the Darwinian law of the disappearance of the weakest still finds its application.

In democratic countries, as we now know them, it is useless to place one's hope in the struggle of the State *versus* private capital. The struggle cannot exist as the State is in the hands of the capitalists. In Germany on the contrary, the fascist party was strong enough to take control to a large extent, of the State and impose sacrifices on the capitalist class.   If, therefore, the *New Statesman and Nation* wants to find a country where compulsion is applied by the State it has only to look to Germany.

The extraordinary ignorance of the pro-war "socialists" as to the nature of fascism makes them want to fight fascism with exactly fascist methods.   We, who are often accused of not opposing fascism in an effective way, want, on the contrary, to fight it with means that have not a fascist nature.   We do not want a fascist State to control both workers and capitalists, we want to abolish the State which is always an instrument of domination of one class over another.   We want the workers to control the land and the factories as well as the means of distribution, so that they will always be able to defend their rights.   This will be the safest way of abolishing any kind of totalitarianism, fascist or democratic.

April, 1941.

15. RECORD OF THE THIRD INTERNATIONAL

AFTER THE collapse of the Second International at the outbreak of
war in 1914, but before the Russian Revolution, Lenin had suggested
the formation of a new International of revolutionary socialist groups
who opposed the war on the grounds of class struggle, but it was not
until 1919 that the Third International was formed in Moscow. From
the start it was made clear that the new International was to
be dominated by the Bolsheviks, and for this reason it was opposed
by many among the Marxists, including Rosa Luxembourg. She sent
Eberlein as German delegate to the preliminary conference with
instructions to vote against the formation of such an International.
But before the conference began Rosa Luxembourg and Karl Lieb-
knecht had been murdered and Eberlein, under pressure, withdrew
his opposition.

Affiliation to the International was conditional on absolute acceptance of the famous 21 points. These made the 3rd International
the most centralised authoritarian body ever formed. Every party
which joined had to submit its programme for the approval of the
Executive Committee in Moscow, (Point 15), while Point 16 laid it
down that decisions of not only world congresses but also of the
Executive Committee, should overrule decisions of the national parties.
Furthermore, the international structure of the national Communist
Parties was prescribed. Hence by its very constitution the national
C.P.s were absolutely tied to Moscow. Right from the beginning the
Bolsheviks would draft decisions for these parties and require their
"leaders" merely to sign on the dotted line.

That absolute control over Communist Parties in all countries
was Lenin's aim is shown clearly by this constitution. But it was
also shown in practice. Independent revolutionists who refused to
submit to the dictatorship of Moscow were discredited by all kinds
of calumnies, while the Comintern welcomed all kinds of servile place
hunters. One of the most glaring examples is that of the French
Communist Marcel Cachin. His case also shows to what extent
the securing of power in Russia had made Lenin modify his original
aim of an international of revolutionary organisations which had
opposed the war.

In 1914 Cachin had been one of the most violently patriotic of
the French Right Wing Socialists. He had acted as agent of the

Allied governments in making overtures to Mussolini to induce him
to come out in the Socialist paper *Avanti* in support of the Allies.
Later, Cachin had been sent by the French Government to persuade
the Russian workers to continue the war.   Cachin was nevertheless
appointed leader of the French C.P., and in 1921 was made a member
of the Executive Committee of the Communist International.

The authoritarianism of the Comintern and the dishonest
methods it employed, not only attracted the most servile and careerist
elements in the working-class movements, but thoroughly disgusted
the genuine, sincere revolutionaries.   The Italian socialist Serrati
refused to commit the Italian Party to the decisions of a handful of
Russians in Moscow: he was vilified with every kind of calumny.
In a letter to Lenin, written in 1920, he declared:

"Your party has six times as many members now as before the
Revolution, but notwithstanding the strict discipline and frequent
purges, it has not gained much as far as quality is concerned.   Your
ranks have been joined by all the slavish elements who always serve
the powerful.   These elements constitute a blind and cruel bureau-
cracy which is creating new privileges in Soviet Russia.   Those
elements which became revolutionary on the day after the Revolution
have made of the Proletarian Revolution which cost the masses so
much suffering, a source of enjoyment and domination."*

The effect of this extreme centralisation coupled with attacks
on all independent revolutionists who refused to be dominated by
the Bolsheviks, was to demoralise the revolutionary movements all
over the world.

Lenin justified the structure and behaviour of the Comintern on
the grounds of the "necessity for stern discipline for the bringing
about of the revolution".   A brief survey of its activity during the
major revolutionary crisis of the past two decades will suffice to show
how it worked in practice.

In 1923 German capitalism was tottering from the repercussions
of the war and the inflation.   In this most important of potential
revolutionary situations the policy of the Comintern was expressed
in Stalin's letter to Bukharin and Zinoviev: "In my opinion the
Germans must be curbed, and not pushed on."   The Executive

*Quoted in *My Life as a Rebel*, by Angelica Balabanoff.

Committee ordered the German Communist leader, Brandler, at this time when Governmental authority was held in contempt by the German workers, actually to enter the Social Democratic Government of Saxony.

In 1927 revolutionary feeling was so high in China that the peasants in many districts expropriated the land and formed peasant soviets. At the same time the industrial workers carried out the most militant strikes in the principal cities. The Comintern ordered the Chinese Communists to discourage the formation of soviets, and to bury their arms. In this way it disarmed the revolutionists and abandoned them to the tender mercies of Chiang Kai-Shek to be literally massacred. These moves of the Comintern won the approval of the capitalist countries and offered prospects of fruitful collaboration with Stalin. The American ex-Ambassador to Russia, J. Davies, declared recently:

"As far back as 1938, I was reliably informed in Moscow that the Soviet Union was most helpful to the Government of General-issimo Chiang Kai-Shek, in that it exercised its influence on behalf of the Chinese Government to prevent communistic activities which would impair the common defence against Japan. That is indicative of the kind of decent co-operation which in my opinion, can be expected from the Soviet Government in the interests of a peaceful world."

But in 1936 a far more important situation arose. On July 19th the Spanish workers organised the armed resistance to Franco. Here, surely, was the opportunity for a so-called revolutionary International to show its capabilities. What happened? The Russian Government, as André Gide showed, gave the minimum of publicity in its papers to the fact that the Spanish revolution had ever occurred. Russia was the first power to sign the Non-Intervention Agreement. Meanwhile the national sections of the Comintern were unanimous in declaring that so far from a revolution having taken place in Spain, the Spanish workers were fighting for bourgeois democracy! Later the agents of the Comintern devoted their energies not to fighting Franco at the front, but to assassinating revolutionists behind the lines, while Communist Brigades destroyed the work of the peasant and workers collectives. The Comintern in Spain acted as the instrument of counter-revolution and devoted its energies to destroying the achievements of the Revolution.

In every revolutionary situation which confronted it the Comintern managed to destroy the revolutionary forces and demoralize the working-class.   Have they any better record in the day-to-day resistance to the class enemy?

Quite early in its history, the allegedly revolutionary aims of the Comintern stood in contrast to the diplomatic relations of the Soviet Union with other countries.

Thus the Bolsheviks entered into commercial agreements with Mussolini's Fascist Government soon after it assumed power in Italy. On the morning after the murder of the Socialist deputy Matteotti the Soviet Ambassador called on Mussolini.   At the very same time when the German Communists were planning the overthrow of the State, the Russian government was not only making trade agreements with the German capitalist government, but even making secret arrangements whereby the Germans could evade the military terms of the Treaty of Versailles by establishing arms factories, and training armies, on Russian soil.   Wherever a clash occurred the claims of Soviet foreign policy prevailed over the needs of the revolutionary class struggle.

The clearest example of the ineptitude of the Comintern is to be found in its attitude towards Nazism.   As long ago as 1929 they were declaring that, as compared with German Social Democracy, Hitler's National Socialism was the less pernicious.   At a session of the International, D. Z. Manuilsky (whose name now appears on the document dissolving the Comintern), declared that "Fascism of the Hitler type does not represent the chief enemy."   In 1931 the German C.P. actually joined in a campaign to overthrow the predominantly socialist democratic government of Germany.   Even when Hitler came to power in 1933 their slogan continued to be "After Hitler, our turn".   When Stalin wished to form a treaty with France, the Communist Parties were ordered to carry out a Popular Front programme of unity not only with social democrats (formerly stigmatized as "Social Fascists") but with liberals as well.

In 1939, failing a pact with England the Soviet Union made an alliance with Hitler, and the constituent parties of the Third International opposed the war. On the dissolution of that pact in June 1941, they swung to an extreme social patriotic position.

The Comintern has almost from the beginning served primarily, not as an instrument for World Revolution, but as an instrument of Russian Foreign Policy. The rigid control over the national Communist Parties by the Moscow committee has made these parties in effect a powerful Russian Fifth Column in all countries. An important aspect of their functions was the supplying of military information to the Russian Government. In most European countries, Communists have served terms of imprisonment on this kind of charge.

Control over the constituent Communist parties was established in the constitution of the Comintern as laid down by Lenin and Trotsky. Infractions of this discipline resulted in a summons to Moscow and subjection to the supervision of the foreign sections of the GPU. The fate of Willi Muenzenburg, Trotsky and many besides must have had the effect of "encouraging the others". But the Comintern also established a financial strangle-hold upon its national parties which were made absolutely dependent on Moscow. How far this principle was carried is shown by the following example, cited by Jan Valtin.* The Swedish C.P. by means of an efficiently run system of seamen's hostels was able to make itself financially independent. The agents of the Comintern therefore set to work to break up this system and so force the too-independent party into dependence on Moscow.

The Comintern has in fact never been an instrument of revolution. During the last twenty years it has performed the most bewildering changes of policy and political somersaults. Yet throughout this apparent diversity there has remained one consistent thread by which the most contradictory attitudes can be explained. At every turn the Comintern has counted out the needs of Russian foreign policy in relation to capitalist governments.

While cringingly following the commands of the Soviet government, the most brutal and long-standing tyranny of our era, the Comintern throughout its inglorious history has never at any time served the interests of the working class.

June, 1943.

Out of the Night, London, 1941, pp. 318-320.

16. STALINIST OFFENSIVE AGAINST REVOLUTIONARY MILITANTS

AMONGST THE people interested in politics, there are quite a number of Soviet Union sympathisers. The Russian resistance to the German offensive has attracted the attention of a great number of workers, intellectuals and bosses towards a strange and unknown continent which a clever and multifaced propaganda describes simultaneously as a proletarian paradise, a miracle of technical organisation, an example of religious tolerance, as well as being a nation extraordinarily, well armed.

The propaganda agents of the "Friends of the U.S.S.R." are extremely clever in attracting and interesting newcomers. If you are a teacher, the propagandist will talk to you about the new system of education in the Soviet Union. If you are a Catholic he will praise the freedom of religious belief in the U.S.S.R.; if you are an engineer, the Dnieper Dam; if you are a worker, workers' power; if you are a capitalist, the struggle against Hitler who has established state control over everything; if you play chess, the Russian champions; if you are a woman, the equal rights between the sexes; if you are a Jew, the unparalleled liberty which exists for the Jews in the U.S.S.R.

Stalin is successively the protagonist of parachutists, a technician, the Pope's friend, the brother of colonial people, Buddha with multiple arms, or the Trinity; the father of the people, Jesus Christ and spiritual power. He has not yet been portrayed as the Holy Virgin, but that will come in time.

The Communist International needs in each country, a popular embassy for the U.S.S.R. a sector of the population which can be easily manœuvred and which can be made to exert influence on their government. The more ignorant the sympathisers are of the real Soviet Union, of the true nature of the Communist Party, of the work of the G.P.U. all over the world, the better. Those who keep their eyes open are enemies. The Communist Party prefers to attract a bourgeois with whom it is possible to work for a short time because he is without scruple, to a man who uses his brain and says frankly what he thinks. If the man who thinks is also an active revolutionary he can be sure of his fate.

If you happen to be the Dean of Canterbury, or Stafford Cripps, or Roosevelt, you are alright, but if you are an honest revolutionary worker, or intellectual, there's no hope for you. With the first, all compromises are possible, with the latter, it is open war.

That is why the communist offensive has never relaxed in its war against the revolutionary movements and individuals which are a living reproach to the Stalinist betrayal.*

The strength of the Communist Party lies in the ever renewed flow of sympathisers. Some people, however, have a good memory and for them the propaganda of the Friends of the U.S.S.R. is useless. In order to prevent the past from condemning the present, in order to prevent Lenin from judging Stalin, the militiamen from condemning the Stalinist commissars, the communist militants from denouncing the Communist Party, the victims of the G.P.U. from accusing their persecutors, it is necessary to shut their mouths.

Never has the Communist International expended so much effort, so much money and perseverance as they are doing in the offensive against the socialist revolutionaries—the syndicalists and the anarchists, who know and denounce the Soviet lie.

The American continent is at present the theatre of an intensive struggle between the various types of propaganda of the rival imperialisms. Newspapers, radio stations, political parties and trade unions, have become the prey of one or the other capitalist opponent. Hypocritical alliances are made and unmade every day, according to the necessities of the moment between English, American and Russian agents. The only thing they all agree on is to liquidate and suppress the few independent voices which continue to make themselves heard in the midst of the universal madness: those of the revolutionaries who do not wear a uniform.

Each state is taking measures of a fascist character in order to gradually suppress all the liberty of the press, of the spoken word and of organisation, so as to suppress any revolutionary movement.

The Soviet agents collaborate in this suppression with great joy, but raise great howls when the bourgeois try to use the reactionary laws against them. But very often they are not even allowed to protest when their own organisations have to suffer under the methods

*An account of the executions outside Russia ordered by the G.P.U. has recently been published under the title *Assassins at Large*, by Hugo Dewar, London, 1951.—EDITOR.

used by the "democratic" governments. That is why Brazil, denounced by the communists a few months ago as the best organised fascist State in South America, is now considered the best example of democracy.

Chile has become, according to the communists, a nest of fascist conspirators, even though the Chilian C.P. has organised a campaign in favour of its president, Juan Antonio Rios. But at the same time it has organised a long strike in the copper mines of the Braden Copper Co., in connivance with the American government in order to exert their pressure on the president.

In the United States, the Communists are collaborating with the most open reactionaries, so long as they are in favour of helping the U.S.S.R., and the defence of "democracy".

Faithful to their methods of moral dishonesty and police tactics, the propaganda service of the Russian government has launched, in Mexico, a campaign of calumny, and provocation to murder, against all the independent revolutionary elements living in the country.

Some well-known communist agents are directing the business. One of them is André Simone (pseudonym for Otto Katz, agent of the Comintern) another is Comorera, famous for his acts in revolutionary Spain, one of which consisted in starving the Barcelona population in order to put the blame on the syndicates and so destroy workers' control.

Knowing whom we have to deal with we can not be surprised at the style of the G.P.U. methods in Mexico.

One should also note that the Stalinist agitation runs parallel with the reaction of the Mexican bourgeoisie, so that the American capitalists can sleep without fear, on their beds of petrol shares, knowing that the watchful dogs of the Comintern are defending their interests and have taken on the job of calumniating, denouncing or assassinating all revolutionaries who oppose them.

The Spanish anarchists in Mexico are attacked both by the bourgeois press and the Stalinists, who demand that they should be interned in concentration camps. The Spanish anti-fascists who hold the same views now as they did in July 1936, and who have refused to change their ideas like the followers of the Soviet Church, must not be allowed freedom.

The exile who arrives in Mexico does not receive a work permit from the government; the bosses refuse to employ him because they know that he is a militant; the trade unions reject him as a competitor on the labour market. If the emigré is furthermore, a man who thinks, acts and does not bend, he will be insulted, his name dragged through the mud, or if he is important enough, assassinated by Stalin's agents.

There is at present in Mexico (the rest are in the United States, Chile, and Argentine), a well-assorted communist gang. In it are three of the four murderers of Andrés Nin, supported by a few hundred members who have learned their trade in Spain, in France, in the Soviet Tcheka and in the S.I.M. (Spanish Intelligence Service).

The men who are in greatest peril at present are (apart from a small group of C.N.T. militants who have remained faithful to their anarchist ideas and who are grouped round Miguel Yoldi, ex-organiser of the Durruti Column in Aragon and in Madrid), Victor Serge, Gorkin and Marceau Pivert.

Victor Serge is a gifted writer, who took part in the organisation of the Soviets at the beginning of the Russian revolution, and who knows the political and police machinery of the Russian State well. Julian Gorkin was the founder of the Third International in Spain and has experienced prison and exile. He was an old enemy of the G.P.U. and only by a miracle escaped assassination by their agents during the Spanish Revolution. Marceau Pivert, leader of the P.S.O.P., (Workers' and Peasants' Socialist Party) in France is a militant of incontestable political and revolutionary honesty.

A well-organised Press campaign has been raised against these three men, and three Stalinist deputies have denounced them in the Mexican Parliament as leaders of the Fifth Column in Latin-America!

This could be considered as an amusing joke in normal times. But the example of the assassination of Trotsky, and the "suicide" of Krivitsky in the United States, cannot be forgotten, particularly as there are a great number of G.P.U. agents in Mexico. They have plenty of money—which they brought with them from Spain, and are well-armed.

The activity of the refugees in Mexico is open for everybody to see. The articles they write are published in legal newspapers and magazines. The past of most of the militants menaced by the G.P.U. gives the lie to all the communists' accusations. But these men cannot rely on their good faith or on their past in view of the bad faith of the Stalinist agents. They have to rely on the greatest publicity possible being given to the Soviet intrigues, and on the awareness by workers' organisation of these intrigues.

It is up to the workers' organisations to keep a continuous watch on the Stalinist manœuvres, and to eliminate any corruption and intrigue in their midst.

Only by remaining faithful to their revolutionary and international ideals will they be able to resist the Stalinist offensive.

August, 1942.

17. BEHIND THE SLOGANS: FRIENDSHIP WITH THE U.S.S.R.

DELAY IN the arrival of newspapers from foreign countries can cause some surprises at a time when rapid changes in politics require from journalists an ability to alter their 'line' only equalled by the admirers and followers of Holy Russia. The March issue of the American magazine *Life* which has just reached this country offers some interesting reading in the light of the present Anglo-Russian pact. *Life* makes no attempt to conceal the suspicion which exists in America towards Russia and prompts one to wonder how such suspicion can have disappeared in the space of three months as the newspapers want us to believe. While Cripps and most politicians and journalists put the blame for the lack of trust between Britain and Russia, on the British Government, *Life* holds that Russia is responsible for it: "There still exists in a large body of American opinion, a deep suspicion of Russia's purposes. This suspicion is fostered by Axis propagandists, but it has plenty of real basis in the past words and actions of the Soviets".

Life goes on to express fears of a Russian victory:

"It is idle to talk wishfully of Russia and Germany fighting each other to two pulps. In all likelihood one or the other is going to win —this summer. German victory would be a disaster for the U.S.

Russian victory involves dangers and embarrassments which might or might not come true, but there is at least reason to hope that Russia's friends such as Cripps, are right when they say that Stalin has no intention of spreading the Communist system all over Europe. The one way to ensure that this does not happen is for America and Britain to put everything they can muster into the fight. The greater America's contribution to the victory, the greater say America will have in what follows a German defeat on the continent."

This fear to see Russia win does not incline American capitalists to contribute more to victory as *Life* suggests, but leads them to sabotage the shipment of goods to Russia. *Life* goes on to give the following details about the "Aid that doesn't reach Russia":

"So far, America's performance on aid-to-Russia has been apallingly bad . . . The promised quantities have not yet been sent, and Stalin is reported to be 'highly cynical' about American help. In the opinion of some Government officials, the President himself does not know the situation. All the goods promised to Russia have been cleared by the lease-lend authorities, but somewhere along the line they have been held up. Presumably officials, military or civilian, have delayed them, here diverting a shipload of planes to some other destination, there holding a consignment of tanks until the next ship. That 'officials' should be able to indulge in open sabotage of this sort can only mean that they must be sure of receiving protection in high quarters."

From these facts one might conclude that America is really scared that Russia may spread communism to Europe. In reality Americans are extremely well informed as to the nature of the Russian régime. The former Ambassador to Russia, Davies, has apparently been able to enlighten not only Roosevelt, but also Churchill in this respect. They know perfectly well that Stalin is not concerned with spreading the revolution to Europe but he may very well, like Hitler, want to expand his territories and military power. Cripps tried in an article in *Life* to dissipate American suspicions by declaring that Russia after the war will not try to establish socialism in Europe but that Russia wants to reinstate the old balance of power. "I think," he said, "that Russian conception of the post-war world can be summed up by saying that they envisage a world in which the peace is supervised by a strong United States, U.S.S.R., and Great Britain. They were very realistic as to the future, and do not think that mere liberal idealism will serve to keep the peace in a world where the bitterness of the war will take many years to die down and where disarmament on anything like a total scale will not be possible."

It is exactly this realism which is likely to scare the capitalist ruling class. They know perfectly well that in power politics a balance of power is not freely accepted, but must be imposed by circumstances. If the U.S.A., Britain and Russia come out of the war with equal strength then they will have an equal part in "supervising the peace" (euphemism for "ruling the world"). But what if Russia comes out of the war stronger than her allies, will she want to accept them as equal partners? If she were imbued with liberal idealism she might do, but her "realistic" attitude will prevent her from doing so, and she will want to rule Europe.

That American fears have not been dissipated recently is obvious by the incorporation in the Lease-Lend Bill of a clause which restricts Russia from using American material outside her own territory. It is also reasonable to believe that the delay in announcing the signing of the pact by Molotov was due to the fact that he had not yet been to the U.S.A. and that the British Government were waiting to have Roosevelt's opinion. The excuse that Molotov's security demanded secrecy, as newspapers try to suggest, is absurd since it was admitted afterwards that both the House of Commons and Fleet Street knew of the visit. Probably the negotiations which had already taken two months had to be further discussed in the U.S.A. before a final decision could be reached.

Let us denounce all this talk about friendship between the U.S.S.R., America and Britain. There is no such thing as friendship, confidence or trust between powers. Their friendship lies with their interests, as Mr. Molotov who, since the war started, has signed a pact both with Hitler and Churchill, might well testify.

July, 1942.

18. STAKHANOVISM AND THE BRITISH WORKERS

WAR BRINGS a need for increased production and for maximum effort
on the part of the workers.   This is what all the propaganda nowadays tries to impress on the workers.   Since Russia has come into
the war it is not surprising therefore that the Russain worker should
be given as an example to the British workers in order to induce them
to produce more.   The Russian Trade Union delegation in all its
speeches stressed the fact that production could be increased and that
workers in Russia produce far more than they do here.   The influence
of Russian methods is already felt.   The *Manchester Guardian* of
8/3/42 under the heading "Stakhanovites in Lancashire" printed the
following report:

"The Cotton Board's 'Trade Letter' reports the interesting
methods adopted by one firm of cotton spinners and manufacturers to
increase output.   Production boards, especially floodlit have been
set up in all rooms to show daily production and production aimed
at.   Special badges are being made for wear by operatives with good
or increased output records.   These badges have a design of the
firm's crest with the words 'War Production Worker'.

Weekly five-minute 'pep-talks' are being given through microphones while the workers have meals in the canteen.   A weekly or
fortnightly letter to the operatives is being compiled to keep them
in touch with all the latest developments."

Production boards and badges—these are familiar methods of
stimulating the Russian workers but, since the introduction of Udarn-
ism and Stakhanovism, the Russian Government has gone much further
in its technique of increasing production.   If Russian methods are
going to be introduced in this country it may be of interest to the
British workers to know what these methods really consist of.

According to Stalin, socialism can and will defeat the capitalist
system "Because it can furnish higher models of labour, a higher
productivity of labour than the capitalist system of economy.   Because
it can give society more products and can make society richer than
the capitalist system can."   The aim of the Russian revolution has
not been as one would have expected to reduce the working hours
of the worker and to improve his standard of living but to make him

produce more and more. Stakhanovism was not the first method used by the ruling classes of the Soviet Union to extract more work from the people. Already in 1928 brigades of udarniks were formed. The udarniks being workers who voluntarily undertook to work more and better, "to set themselves to raise the standard of output, to diminish scrap or breakages, to put an end to time wasting or unnecessary absenteeism, and to make the utmost of the instrument of socialist emulation." (*Soviet Communism* by S. & B. Webb). Udarniks received all kinds of privileges in food, clothes and holidays which put them in a superior position to that of the rest of the workers. Piece-work being general in Russia they also, of course, received better salaries.

Udarniks received, like stakhanovists later, the greatest publicity and encouragement from the government; but such publicity cannot have an everlasting effect and in 1935 a new publicity campaign was launched with the introduction of Stakhanovism. In May 1935, Stalin made a speech telling the younger workers of the U.S.S.R. that they must "master technique". This was the signal for the campaign for increased production, and in August of the same year the miner Stakhanov, with the help of the communist directors of the mine, established the first record of cutting 100 tons of coal in one day (the average coal cut in the Ruhr is 10 tons and the maximum 16 or 17 tons per day). All over Russia and in every kind of industry, from cotton weavers to shop assistants and trade union officials, Stakhanovists sprang up. The Government insisted on the spontaneity of the movement and explained it by the improvement in the conditions of the workers but it was obvious that it was inspired and supported by the whole governmental machine. Stakhanov's declaration praising Stalin as the originator of the movement can be taken literally rather than as a compliment to the leader: "I really do not know why this movement is called the Stakhanovtchina it should be rather the Stalintchina (Stalin's movement)! The beloved leader of the Communist Party and of the peoples of the U.S.S.R., comrade Stalin and the Bolshevik party which he leads have inspired our victories."

The purpose behind the Stakhanovist campaign soon became obvious. The Central Committee declared that the enthusiasm shown by the workers was due to the betterment of their conditions of life and instead of rejoicing at this improvement immediately proceeded to decree the revision of all norms of work.

A revision of collective labour contracts was carried out which resulted in the increasing of the norms of work without a corresponding increase in wages and in the creation of a labour caste receiving higher wages and privileges. A Stakhanovist miner received 580 roubles in 11 days instead of a month. A Stakhanovist engine driver received 900 roubles a month instead of 400, etc. This created hostility and division amongst the workers.

The Stakhanovist method is not something new. Ford and Taylor had long before defined means by which the workers would produce the maximum work in the minimum time. Their methods were of course despised and hated by the working people all over the world. When a few years ago the Duke of Windsor wanted to visit an American factory in the company of Bedaux, the workers threatened to go on strike if he came with the man who had refined the methods of exploitation of the workers. The originality of the Russian method was to give a character of spontaneity to the movement, of covering the dirty exploitation of the majority of the workers under a heap of socialist slogans. Stakhanovist workers did not find new methods of work, they rationalised production somehow by introducing more division of labour. Stakhanov for example was helped by a team which prepared the place and removed the coal while he concentrated on cutting coal. Stakhanovist salesmen quickened their service "by having already packed the quantities usually demanded of the commodities in greatest request." (*Soviet Communism*, S. & B. Webb)

The records achieved by Stakhanovist workers were obviously tricked (gangs worked at night in order to prepare the work, a gang of workers assisted the Stakhanovist, etc.). This explains how certain Stakhanovist workers have achieved records which have met with the incredulity of most western workers. Two months after Stakhanov cut 102 tons of coal in one day, for example, the miner Matchekin cut in the same time 1,466 tons of coal! The Government did not take the trouble to explain these figures—it merely wanted to impress the imagination of the average worker, make him feel ashamed of the little work he did. One should mention here that after having achieved these records most Stakhanovists were taken into rest houses, or were sent to lecture in Universities and factories. They did not go back to work, their job was done; they had proved that workers could produce more. In April 1936, an Institute of Work which prepared norms compatible with maintaining good health among the workers was closed as harmful, its scientific norms having been brilliantly demolished by Stakhanovist practice!

As might be expected, the already overworked and underfed Russian workers did not accept with enthusiasm an increase in the norms of production which for many meant a reduction of wages. The Soviet Press reported many cases where Stakhanovists met with the hostility of their fellow workers.

"In the factory Krasny Schtampovtchik, a Stakhanovist worker found on her loom a dirty broom with the following note: 'To the comrade Belog, this bouquet is offered in order to thank her for having increased by three times our norms'." (*Troud* 1/11/35)

" 'Horses are not men; they cannot follow socialist emulation'. This is what Maximovitch had the audacity to say to Orloff, an official of the Communist Youth, who proposed that he increase the work of horse conductors at the bottom of the mine. When we asked how was the (Stakhanovite) method carried out in Loutch we learned by a local paper that out of 38 pits 35 opposed the new method with a more or less open sabotage." (*Izvestia* 2/10/35)

In a factory where wagons were being repaired two workers were condemned to five and three years imprisonment respectively for having stolen the tools of a Stakhanovist worker. (*Pravda* 2/11/35).

The locksmith Konovalov killed the super-udarnik Rachtepa. (*Izvestia* 23/8/35).

"The military tribunal has condemned the murderers of the Stakhanovist Schmirev, the brothers Kriachkiv, to the highest punishment for social offence, to be shot." (*Pravda* 21, 22/11/35).

Outside Russia the Stakhanovist movement was praised only by the communist and russophile press. Workers looked with mixed feelings of amusement and indignation at the 'records' of Stakhanovist workers in Russia. A French miner, Kleber Legay, denounced the dangerous conditions in which Russian miners accomplished these exploits. In France, communist leaders had to write to their communist newspapers to stop publication of records achieved by Stakhanovist workers as they were received with laughter by the French miners. The word Stakhanovist was used by many as an insult!

The Stakhanovist movement is, according to the Webbs:

"a revolution in the wage-earners mentality towards measures and devices for increasing the productivity of labour . . . (because) . . . in soviet industry, there is no 'enemy party' . . . the manual worker in the factory . . . realises that the whole of the aggregate net product . . . is genuinely at the disposal of the aggregate workers . . . in such ways as they by their own trade organisation, choose to determine."

The Stakhanovist movement is nothing of the sort. It is a method whereby a minority of workers stronger or more skilled than others receive a higher salary and privileges at the expense of other workers. The factory management could afford to pay Stakhanovist workers more than others because they helped to raise the norms of production and therefore lowered the wages of the other workers. As Taylor had already pointed out: "one must pay high salaries in order to have cheap labour".

If the workers in the Soviet Union really believed that by working harder they would increase "the whole of the aggregate product at the disposal of the aggregate workers" there would have been no need to encourage them to produce more by according special privileges to them. Furthermore by paying Stakhanovist workers more the Government made it plain that the aggregate product was not going to benefit equally each worker but only a minority.

The only difference between Stakhanovism and the old methods of capitalist exploitation consists in the fact that the workers are made to believe that they are not exploited at all but are, in reality, working for the building up of a socialist state. Workers are asked to stop defending their wages and trying to decrease their hours of work and to put the interest of the State before their own.

In Russia the workers are asked to do this under the pretext of building up a Socialist Country while in reality it is not Socialism which is built on worker's sweat but a class of bureaucrats and politicians. In this country workers are asked to help the Government to produce more, in spite of the capitalist system of economy, so that the war can be won quicker. In both cases the workers are asked to defend interests which are not theirs. Socialism is achieved in the factories and in the fields by the workers taking over production and distributing the products according to peoples' needs. It is not achieved by dividing the working class in categories of wage earners, by applying degrading methods of production: piece-work and a sweating system.

When, with the pretext of fighting Fascism, British workers are asked to collaborate with the capitalists and the Government to carry out their own exploitation by such means as setting up production committees or by introducing Stakhanovist methods, they should remember that Fascism is fought more efficiently in the factories than on the battlefields. Every defeat of the capitalist class is a defeat for fascism. Every time the workers obtain a reduction in their hours of work and a rise in salaries, every time they affirm workers' solidarity by defending a victimized fellow worker, every time they achieve a victory over their boss, they win a victory against Fascism and pave the way to socialism.

When the revolution has been achieved there will be no need for Stakhanovist methods. All workers will give society labour according to their strength and ability, not in exchange for wages but for food, clothes, and pleasures, to satisfy their needs.

March, 1942.

19. STALIN BEATS BEVIN. LABOUR CONSCRIPTION IN U.S.S.R.

THE NEWSPAPERS reported on the 16th of April that Russia's railways had been placed under martial law. The reason given being the usual one of preventing sabotage "by an unimportant minority of irresponsible workers". The six points of the new decree by Stalin are:—

1.—All railways are under martial law; 2.—All railway workers are fully mobilised and are unable to leave their jobs; 3.—Railway workers are to be held responsible for offences or failures in their work in the same way as soldiers; 4.—Offences are to be tried by war tribunals; 5.—Offenders will be dismissed and sent to serve on the front unless tribunals pass more severe sentences; 6.—The Peoples' Commissar for Transport Kaganovich and managers of the railways have power to place offenders under administrative arrest for periods up to 21 days.

To appreciate the severity of the decree one has to bear in mind how strict is the discipline to which the Red Army soldier is subjected. This new ukase by Stalin however, is only in the tradition of the Bolshevik Government. Ever since the revolution the Russian worker has been subjected, except during short intervals, to military discipline. Trotsky had already in 1918 gone far in the direction towards militarising industrial workers. The peasants' lot was no better. In 1919, to the decree ordering the requisition of their goods was added the obligation to provide forced labour and transport. At the end of the civil war the workers' opposition to militarisation increased, but new orders were issued in October 1920, for a mobilisation of labour on military lines accompanied by the typical Bolshevik instructions that it should be affected "with revolutionary animation". In 1930 and 1931 a crisis in railway transport was solved by compulsory recall to transport service of persons having technical experience. Again compulsion was used to secure skilled labour for timber floating in the spring thaw.

Legislation similar to the Essential Works Order in this country existed in Russia long before the present war started. The Russian law "provides a reserve power of complete industrial conscription, which requires that in case of public crisis everyone between the ages of eighteen and forty-five in the case of men (and forty in the case of women) must take part in work required by the Government except only women more than seven months advanced in pregnancy, nursing mothers and women with young children who have no one to look after them" (*Labour Code of the Russian Federal Republic*, quoted by the Webbs in *Soviet Communism*).

A decree of October, 1930, introduced compulsory transfer of labour; skilled workmen in non-essential industries could be directed into coal mining or into the building industry. Railway technicians had to go wherever they were directed. Maynard, in the *Russian Peasant: and other Studies*, quotes several examples from the Soviet Statute book where compulsory labour was used: —

"In the spring of 1930, there is to be 'rigorous discipline in connection with timber-floating, after the thaw', and labour is to be despatched from collective farms to 'seasonal branches of the national economy-construction, floating, agriculture, loading and unloading' Demands of labour for loading and unloading of grain, and of export and import goods, are to have priority: and all unemployed persons (this refers to 1930) are to obey the call, for work on these tasks, on pain of deprivation of unemployment benefit. Intellectual workers are included in this order. Labour organisations are to create voluntary brigades of shock-workers to work off accumulations of unloading and loading . . . the system of agreements with collective farms for use of their surplus labour involves a measure of compulsion upon individuals."

Children do not escape labour conscription. The Press announced on the 6th of May, 1941, that a decree ordering the mobilisation of 700,000 boys and girls between the ages of 14 and 17 as labour reservists had been issued in Moscow. They were to be in addition to the five millions already mobilised for training in trade schools as skilled industrial workers. A decree of October, 1940, had already restricted the choice of employment by young people. Those in collective farms were chosen by the Committee and obliged to undergo industrial training and remain for a certain period in the trade to which they had been directed.

In view of the number of decrees ordering compulsory labour it is surprising to see that Beatrice and Sidney Webb deny the existence of compulsion in Russia. In *Soviet Communism* they declare:

"Unless we are to consider as slavery all work done for wages or salary, in pursuance of contracts voluntarily entered into, and upon conditions settled by trade unions in collective bargaining, there does not seem to be any implication of slavery involved in a planned economy. The Government of the U.S.S.R. has, indeed, no need to employ compulsion to fill its factories or state farms, or even its lumber camps."

This statement is contradicted by the Webbs themselves who, a few lines earlier, referred to "the forced removal from their homesteads to other districts, leading normally to less pleasant opportunities of earning their living, of kulaks and other recalcitrants who in 1931-1932 obstructed the formation of collective farms or the timely sowing and reaping".

One might question the validity of contracts entered into by the Russian Trade Unions in the name of the workers. Even if the Central Committee of Trade Unions had given its consent to the labour decrees ordering compulsion, these are nevertheless forced upon the workers. The Russian Trade Unions are merely the instruments of the State and their decisions are not reached by the rank and file members. It would be just as absurd to say that in this country the Essential Works Order is a voluntary contract between the Government and the workers when the workers were never consulted and when the entire Emergency Regulations controlling the country at the present time were passed by the House of Commons in less than two hours, receiving the support of M.P.s who confessed afterwards that they had had no time to read them.

Not only compulsory labour exists in Russia, but slave labour, too. With the excuse of punishing them for their opposition to the Government, millions of people have been, during the last fifteen years, condemned to penal labour. An immense army of men and women has been formed whom the Government can direct to do the hardest work without payment of wages and who are kept at starvation level. It was after the decree ordering the collectivisation of the land in 1929 that the Government first experimented in the use of penal labour on a big scale. Peasants who opposed the decree were arrested by the G.P.U. (the Red Army is said to have refused to do the job for fear of revolt in its ranks) and transported to build roads and canals. Since the decree met with great opposition in the countryside, the Government was able to draw from an almost inexhaustible supply of labour: —

"Before long, Dnieperstroi, Magnitostroi, every important construction job, had its crowded barracks for the deported kulaks, virtual prisoners of the State, as well as for the actual convicted prisoners who were locked in at the end of the working day."

—(Eugene Lyons *Assignment in Utopia.*)

For a time the Press, both in Russia and abroad, denied the use of forced labour by the Russian Government. But when the U.S.S.R. started exporting Soviet goods in 1930 at ridiculously low prices, foreign capitalists became alarmed and something became known about conditions in the Soviet labour camps. Eugene Lyons, who was in Russia at the time, exposes in his book the lies used at the time both by the Soviet Government and the foreign journalists: —

"The Soviet government's denials of forced labour put the finishing touches on the diverting Olympiad of hypocrisy involved in the 'anti-dumping' campaign. 'Prisoners everywhere work, why should not ours?' the Kremlin asked indignantly, thus evading the issue, which was why the U.S.S.R. possessed so many hundreds of thousands of prisoners. It did not explain whether a million or so men and women transported forcibly to places where there was only one job and one employer and then given a free choice of employment were 'forced labour' or not.

"For the special purpose of appeasing American public opinion, an American 'commission' was dispatched to the lumber area and in due time it attested truthfully that it had not seen forced labour . . . I knew all three men intimately, and it is betraying no secret to record that each of them was . . . thoroughly convinced of the widespread employment of forced labour in the lumber industry . . . they placated their conscience by merely asserting ambiguously that they personally had seen no signs of forced labour; they did not indicate that they made no genuine effort to find it and that their official guide steered the 'investigation'."

Forced labour, with its indescribable sufferings and hardships, has found its apologists. Louis Fisher has described the army of slaves of the G.P.U. as a "vast industrial organization and a big educational institution." The G.P.U., in fact, found itself able to employ millions of people with a minimum of expense. No wonder the G.P.U. soon prospered and became one of the biggest contracting firms in the country, being able to undertake anything from the manufacture of a camera to the building of roads and canals. Maurice Edelman, in *How Russia Prepared,* explains how the prisoners of the G.P.U. were not allowed to decay in idleness: —

"Road building is controlled by the Central Highway Administration of the People's Commissariat for Home Affairs—translated into Russian, the G.P.U. . . . At a time of great social change, when resistance to such change was an offence, the dissidents whom the G.P.U. interned numbered many hundreds of thousands. They were not allowed to decay in idleness. The internees were put to the task of improving Soviet communications, particularly by road and canal."

The G.P.U. saw to it that there was plenty of labour available for its various enterprises:

" . . . from the isolated official admissions by the government.(at least 200,000 prisoners engaged on the Baltic-White Sea Canal, several hundred thousand in double-tracking the Trans-Siberian Railroad, etc.), a conservative estimate of the total at the time when Fisher's "vast industrial organisation' was at its vastest would be two millions. If we add the exiled peasants transported to areas under G.P.U. supervision . . . the total would at least be tripled."—(Eugene Lyons).

The immense armies of slave labour of the G.P.U have no parallel in any other country in the world. What exists in a sporadic way and on a small scale in countries like India or China has been organized along the most ruthless and efficient lines by the Soviet State. And yet forced labour in the camps of the G.P.U., where people die of hunger and cold, submitted to the discipline of convicts, treated like animals whom it is unnecessary to spare as ten can take the place of the one who falls, is the logical consequence of laws enforcing military discipline on the workers at the time of the revolution. The artisans of the February and October Revolution gave up their right to organise their work and to run the factories themselves. They allowed the State to impose its discipline upon them. At the time the State was still weak and it had to treat them with a certain amount of respect and consideration. But when it succeeded in crushing its bourgeois enemies from outside and the revolutionary movement in Russia itself, the Bolshevik Government was able to build powerful weapons in order to regiment and suppress the Russian working class. Ten years after the end of the revolution, Stalin's Government was able to use compulsion in industry on a great scale and to reduce millions of peasants to the status of slaves; the greatest achievement in the oppression of peoples known in the history of mankind.

May, 1943.

2

The Price of War and of Liberation

---

20. BRITISH BOMBING

BRITISH BOMBING has brought death to many thousands of people in
the past few weeks. At Quebec, politicians who provide themselves
with shelters well out of reach of bombs, are planning to continue
massive bombing as a means of carrying on the "war against fascism".

Hamburg, Milan, Genoa, Turin, are covered with ruins, their
streets heaped with bodies and flowing with blood. "Hamburgizing"
is coming into use as a new term for wholesale destruction of cities,
and the mass murder of their populations through terrorist raids.
The Press boasts of the R.A.F.'s power to carry such destruction to
all the cities of Germany and Central Europe. It screamed with
indignation when the Germans bombed churches and hospitals, but
when the smell of carnage goes up from once beautiful and populous
towns they find words of rejoicing. When the water mains were
hit in Milan, and the centre of the city was flooded, they find it a
subject for a joke. "Lake Milan" the clever journalist calls it. What
does it matter to him if "the water is flowing between the ruins and
the debris of bombed buildings, and people living in the district
were forced to remain in the wreckage of their homes for four days
until the water subsided and they could get out . . . " "Lake Milan"
is indeed a splendid joke. But while the journalists chuckle in the
Fleet Street pubs, the hospitals and rescue squads are working day
and night to try and palliate some of the pain and disfigurement,
the hunger and exposure of the victims.

Our cartoonists also find wholesale destruction a matter for humorous comment. "Berlin is off the air, and will soon be off the map too!" But when the newspapers publish descriptions and photographs of the destruction and misery in Hamburg and Milan, the people of Clydeside and Coventry, Plymouth and the East End of London, will be reminded of the days and nights when *their* houses were bombed, when their relatives were killed or waited in the hospitals for their turn . . . When the papers talk gloatingly of the streams of refugees frantically pouring out of Hamburg with the remnants of their belongings on their backs, of the people of Milan "camping out under the trees", the people of England's bombed cities will remember their own attempts to get away from the night terror, will remember that when they streamed out of Plymouth into the countryside, they found the big houses of the rich closed to them, and they were left to wander without food or shelter.

For who suffers in the big industrial towns when they are bombed, if not the workers who have led lives of misery and toil just like the workers of Clydeside or Coventry? When the port of Naples is bombed, it is the thickly populated working class district which surrounds the harbour that suffers most. The bombs do not hit the sumptuous villas of rich Fascists which are scattered along the shores of the bay of Naples; they hit those high storeyed houses so crowded one on top of the other that the streets are no more than dark passages between them; houses where people live four or five in a room.

When German cities are bombed it is not the Nazi elite which suffers. They have deep and comfortable shelters just like the elite in this country. Their families have been evacuated to safe districts or to Switzerland. But the workers cannot escape. The city proletariat, the French, Dutch, Belgian, and Scandinavian workers are forced by Himmler's factory Gestapo to go on working in spite of the heavy bombing. For them escape is impossible.

Workers in British munition factories and aircraft factories are asked to rejoice at this wholesale destruction from which there is no escaping. Photographs, showing great heaps of ruins, are plastered all over the walls with the caption "This is your work". The ruling class wants them to be proud that they have helped to destroy working class families. For that is what they have done. They have helped their masters to stage massacres compared with which the destruction of Guernica, the bombing of Rotterdam and Warsaw look like playing at war.   Such posters should outrage humanity, make them feel sick at the rôle capitalist society calls upon them to play.

The Italian workers have shown that, in spite of twenty years of fascist oppression, they knew better where their class interests lay. They have refused to be willing tools in the hands of the bosses. They have gone on strike, have sabotaged war industry, have cut telephone wires and disorganized transport. What is the answer of Democratic Britain to their struggle against fascism?   Bombing and more bombing.   The Allies have asked the Italian people to weaken Mussolini's war machine, and we now take advantage of their weakness to bomb them to bits.

Our politicians professed to want revolution in Europe to overthrow fascism.   But it is now clearer than ever that what they are most afraid of is that fascism should be overthrown by popular revolt.   They are terrified of revolution, terrified of "Anarchy". They want to establish "order", and as always they are prepared to wade through rivers of blood to secure their idea of order—order in which the workers accept their lot of poverty and pain with resignation.

How many times in the past have we heard that Anarchism means bombs, that anarchists work for wholesale destruction.   How many times has ruling class police repression been instituted because an anarchist has attempted to assassinate a single ruler or reactionary politician?   But one single Hamburgizing raid kills more men and women and children than have been killed in the whole of history, true or invented, of anarchist bombs.   The anarchist bombs were aimed at tyrants who were responsible for the misery of millions; ruling class bombs just kill thousands of workers indiscriminately.

"Disorder", "Anarchy", cried the bourgeois Press when single-handed resolutes like Sbardelotto, Schirru and Lucetti, tried to kill Mussolini . . .   Now the same capitalists want to rub whole cities off the map of Europe; want to reduce whole populations to starvation, with its resulting scourge of epidemics and disease all over the world.   This is the peace and order that they want to bring to the workers of the world with their bombs.

September, 1943.

21. By Fire and Sword

IN THE PREFACE to the Baedeker for Paris and its surroundings, published in 1881, one finds a description of the "most deplorable recent disasters caused by the fiendish proceedings of the Communists during the second 'reign of Terror', 20th-28th May, 1871". According to the writer "Within that week of horrors no fewer than twenty-two important public buildings and monuments were wholly or partly destroyed, and a similar fate overtook seven railway stations, the four principal public parks and gardens, and hundreds of dwelling-houses and other buildings."

If Baron Karl Baedeker would have had to write a preface to a guide to Paris in the years which will follow the present war he would probably have had to record far more "fiendish" proceedings on the parts of the retreating German army and the victorious bull-dozing, all-levelling armies of "liberation". There will be a difference, however; the scars that Paris, like the other French towns of Caen, Cherbourg and many more will wear will be noble scars of which the French people will be asked to be proud, and it is doubtful if they will receive slighting references, such as those levelled at the Commune, by the generations of guide-writers to come.

It is the privilege of revolutions that the acts of violence to which they give rise have always received the utmost publicity in newspapers, history books, novels, plays, films . . . and even travellers' books. The horrors of war are forgotten or are glorified for the benefit of tourists, like the ruins of Verdun. But everything conspires to keep alive in people's minds the acts of violence which have taken place during revolutions. Ask any French schoolboy what was the most bloody period in the history of France and he will most probably mention the period of the Terror during the French Revolution. A few thousand people were killed during that period, a small number compared with the Napoleonic wars; an infinitesimal figure compared with the casualties in the war of 1914-1918. Yet the French school-boy will know all about the horrors of the French Revolution, the killing of priests and nobles, the death in captivity of Louis the Sixteenth's heir and the beheading of Marie-Antoinette. But he will know nothing about the million dead of the First World War and the hundreds of thousands of children who died of starvation and disease as a result of it.

Revolutions spell wholesale murder and destruction not only to schoolchildren.   How many times have experienced socialist politicians and learned Fabian professors advocated submission and compromise with the ruling class by waving the spectre of bloody revolution in front of the misguided masses?   It was with tears in his eyes that Leon Blum asked the French people not to intervene in the Spanish revolution.   It was in order to "spare lives" that he watched one of the most splendid revolutionary movements suffocated and allowed the Fascist powers to gain military experience to fight a world war. Of course, when the present war started, Leon Blum forgot all his sensitive love for humanity and urged French people to go to the massacre.   As everyone knows revolutions are bloody affairs but to die wholesale for the motherland is called supreme and sublime sacrifice, so that in these cases death does not really count.

One can easily prophesy that after this war there will still be those people to talk about the horrors of the Commune and of the shooting of fascists, capitalists and priests in Spain.   But the bombing of Hamburg, Paris and London; the bombardment of Caen; the sinking of troop-ships; the death in the skies of thousands of young men; the starvation and pestilence devastating scores of countries— these will all be classified as necessary evils, unavoidable curses which humanity must be proud to endure.   Revolutionists once again, will be considered bloodthirsty fellows who had better be kept locked up and if the choice between war and revolution again presents itself, Christians, socialists and communists, no doubt will, on humanitarian grounds, again choose war.

For the benefit of those sensitive souls we give below extracts from recent publications dealing with the effects of large scale bombing.   Vera Brittain, in a pamphlet called *Massacre by Bombing*, gives some facts which should be kept in mind at a time when journalists and politicians are renewing their efforts of attributing to the Nazis a monopoly in wholesale destruction and massacre.

The pamphlet states that while 50,000 British civilians have been killed by raids in this country, according to German sources, 1,200,000 civilians have been killed or were "missing" in air raids carried out by the Allies on Germany from 1939 to October 1st, 1943.

The "rate of delivery" of bombs dropped by the Allies has increased almost tenfold and is going on increasing.   It has passed from 17½ tons a minute on Cologne in May 1942 to 120 tons a minute in recent raids (80 times the intensity of the heaviest attack ever made on London).

The horror of such bombing cannot be compared with anything we have experienced in this country. The fires started by this intensive bombing suck up so much oxygen that people in nearby shelters are asphyxiated. In Hamburg nearly 20,000 perished that way, suffocated and burnt in their shelters; those who tried to escape from these death-traps were burnt alive: "Women and children in light summer clothing who emerged from the cellars into the storm of fire in the streets were soon converted into human torches."

An account of the bombing of Leipzig has been given by the American magazine *Life* (15/5/44) which publishes a report by three American girls who lived there all through the bombing of the city. In an introductory note *Life* says that:

"By Feb. 21 the German city of Leipzig (pop. 700,000) had been effectively 'obliterated' by Allied bombing. Some 90% of the city installations were said to have been destroyed. Four heavy raids had done the job—three night attacks by British planes; one daylight raid by U.S. Fortresses and Liberators. It was the first time a city of this size had been destroyed by air-power."

This is how the girls described the raid which took place on 19th February:

"I was barely inside the door when the bombs came. They were very near. There weren't just a few of them, but a whole bunch all together. From then on, for nearly an hour, they came incessantly.

The noise was just beyond words. The house shook and shook. First it would sway from side to side, then it would sort of jump, then it would sway and jump together. My knees kept bouncing up and down off the floor.

We never seemed to hear waves of planes, they were just there all the time, all at once. This time we were sitting, holding each other tight with our heads down on our chests. I couldn't really think at all, but I remember once hearing Christina yell: 'There's a bomb coming, open your mouths!' She had seen or read somewhere that soldiers open their mouths when they fire off cannon.

It had never been this bad before. The house was like rubber, bending back and forth, the floor rising up and down like waves.

Nobody talked, nobody screamed. It was quiet as a mouse in the cellar except for the bombs. Even the children were quiet. The people just sat there with their heads bowed, looking as though they were praying . . .

Sometime then I realized that it should have been daylight outside but it wasn't. All that day the sun never got through the smoke and soot and ashes flying through the air. It was twilight all the time, a sort of yellowish brown twilight that stung your eyes and your throat as you breathed . . . Later that day we went out to check on the city . . . there were fires everywhere. At least two houses were burning on every street we came through, usually many more. I had to make one detour after another where streets were completely blocked. It was very difficult walking, piles of rubbish everywhere, people streaming along the streets out of town, many still fighting fires, others carrying things, still others digging for the dead."

The bombing of Germany which is supposed to demoralise the German people and bring them to their knees has the opposite effect. The report in *Life* says that the people of Leipzig displayed courage during and after the bombing and that the anger they felt brought them to give greater support to the war:

"The city looked destroyed, in ruins, but the people were alive and building up again with what they had. They were doing it, too, in a mood of anger and with a sense of companionship that actually gave the people a higher morale than before the bombs fell."

The bombing seems also to have increased the popularity of the Nazi Party:

"The organisations for bomb-damage worked wonders. It was all in the hands of the Party and the work of these organisations won the Party a lot of prestige again. It was all done about as quickly as it could possibly be done and people were taken care of in some way at least right away, even if only with tents and field kitchens."

There are still people who find words of indignation every time a church or a hospital is hit by Nazi bombs. They seem to forget that the destruction carried out by the Allies in their war of liberation aims at the destruction of whole towns and villages. While the armies of the French Revolution were followed up by the overthrow of tyrants and the armies of the Russian Revolution conquered their enemies by fraternizing with them; while the militia columns of the Spanish revolution left behind them expropriated estates and active peasant collectives, the armies of the Allies everywhere bring wholesale destruction and massacre. The recent headlines of a daily paper epitomized the whole character of this war: "BULLDOZERS ARE KEPT BUSY AS WE ADVANCE."

The towns of Messina, Leghorn, Caen, Cherbourg are typical of hundreds of other towns similarly destroyed during the German retreat and the Allied advance.

The *Manchester Guardian* described the destruction of Messina in its issue of 29/5/44:

"When the war left Messina behind it, the city was examined by experts, who pronounced it 94 per cent. uninhabitable. It had been subjected to months of aerial bombardment, culminating in a terrific hammering during the last days of the Sicilian campaign with a view to interfering with the evacuation of the German troops.

No fewer than 10,483 bomb bursts had been counted in the residential quarters of the town, not to mention the port. Afterwards it was heavily bombarded by German guns across the Straits, but the buildings of Messina are of especially strong construction. After the earthquake in 1908 the city was rebuilt of reinforced concrete calculated to resist many times the stresses for which architects normally provide. Consequently, although almost every house was rendered roofless and shattered internally, the outer shell stood firm under bombardment."

The state in which the Allies found Caen is described in the *Manchester Guardian* (10/7/44):

"Caen after more than a month of bombing and shelling, is a dead city and bulldozers have been moved up to prepare a path through the rubble for the tanks.

One officer at the Command Post was so excited that he kept referring to Caen as Cassino. He was not very far wrong as far as the rubble is concerned. Caen is a devastated city; even the trees were flattened and the buildings were unrecognisable as human habitations. Lebisey itself is not much better and the stench of death is heavy over the town. Even some British dead from D-Day are still

lying about. The Germans evidently had no time to bury them as
they had been under almost constant bombardment for the last month.
The prisoners were unshaven, dirty, smelly, and obviously glad to
be out of the war at last."

One could multiply the quotations. Every day newspapers carry
fresh news and heart-breaking photographs showing the heavy toll
this war is taking of human life and dwellings. In Italy the population hid in hovels in the mountains during the Allied advance and
returned later to find their homes destroyed. In Caen the inhabitants
took refuge in ill-smelling caves and the crowded cathedral. Hovels,
caves, roofless houses. These are the places in which this war has
condemned millions of people to live; often they had insufficient food
and water supplies and as a result are easy prey to epidemics.

And this war has been accepted as a "lesser evil" . . .

August, 1944.

22. "LIBERATING" ITALY WITH BOMBS

THE CONQUEST of Italy has started. By adopting methods of blitz-
krieg even superior to those of Germany the Allies have forced the
island of Pantelleria to surrender. Though we have been told for
months that Italy was the unwilling partner of the Axis, that the
morale of the Italian people was very low and that at the sight of
a British soldier whole Italian divisions surrender, thus giving us
the impression that Italy would fall like a pack of cards, we see that
the Allies took no risks in their first attempt to land on Italian soil.
They have shown that they were going to use brute force on as large
a scale as possible.

The *Daily Worker* tried to attribute the defeat to the morale of
the population. In its editorial of June 12, it says: "But the sudden
collapse is not only a tribute to the destructive power of the aerial
attack, it also reveals a breakdown in morale". From the newspaper
reports one can see however that the Allies did not reckon on the
morale of the adversary breaking down. The work was more that
of butchers than of psychologists. Alex Clifford in the *Sunday*

Dispatch describes the island after the surrender: "Landing parties stepped ashore on heaps of rubble which used to be jetties . . . 6,000 civilians were on the island. They had been without water for three days . . . The island, as we landed, was still filled with smoke and fumes from that terrible raid when the entire place disappeared under a boiling pall of smoke. A huge oil dump was burning fiercely near the town. *There are so many bomb holes that sometimes three or four are on top of one another.* This island was beaten into insensibility by its bombing ordeal".

This is how the liberation of Italy has started and there is no reason to think that other methods will be used till the whole country is reduced to submission. There is, it is true, President Roosevelt's appeal and we are assured by the *Sunday Dispatch* New York reporter that "similar calls in between the mass bombings will be made". Those appeals calling on the Italian people to revolt against their government, and dropped to the sound of bombs, are an insult to all intelligent Italians. Government propaganda has, since Italy came into the war, ridiculed the Italian people, treating them as cowards, as a sub-human race good only for the circus. Now those cowardly buffoons are expected to make a revolution under a hail of Allied bombs!

Italian soldiers had to be sneered and laughed at. If the Government did not teach the British people to despise them, who knows, the British tommy might have begun to think that there must be a reason why the Italian did not fight—that he had nothing to fight for, and he might even have begun to wonder if he had anything to fight for himself. It would not have taken him long to realise that the "cowardice" of the Italian people is simply their unwillingness to fight in a cause which is not theirs. Italy, like Spain, is one of the few European countries which had not, till recently, been militarized by an efficient and modern state. She was dragged against her will into the first world war. The anarchist movement and most of the socialist party remained faithful to their anti-militarist ideals; they had a strong influence on the masses who, not being able to prevent the war, did all they could in order to sabotage it.

Since Mussolini's rise to power the Italian people showed that they did not share the Duce's desire for an Italian Empire; they fought badly in Abyssinia. The Abyssinian war was unpopular in Italy

and it was only after the democratic powers adopted their silly policy
of sanctions that Mussolini received some support. In Spain, again,
the Italian soldiers did as little fighting as they could and the Press
sneered at the cowards of Guadalajara. But that "cowardice" had
nothing to do with race or nationality was actually proved on the
Spanish front. On Franco's side were the troops of the Duce, well
equipped, well protected by aviation and tanks; on the other side
fought many Italian anti-fascists, coming from all parts of the world
after exhausting years of exile, with few and obsolete arms. While
the Fascist Italian Divisions gave up their rifles, the Italian anti-
fascists often fought with the rifle of the fallen comrade, and hundreds
of them died on the Aragonese front, glad to give their lives for a
cause to which they had already sacrificed so much.

One has not to go far to find the reason for the lack of enthusiasm of the Italian troops. After twenty or more years of a fascist
régime which has only imposed more and more privations on the
majority of the people, Italians are called on to defend an Empire
which has brought them only wars and sacrifices. Who is called up?
Not the factory worker whose position has been somewhat bettered
under fascism; the industrial worker must remain in the factories to
maintain the supply of war materials. As in all agricultural countries
it is from the peasant population that the majority of the Army is
drawn. From people who have been more and more taxed since
fascism has come to power, who have had to endure the hated interference of the State every minute of their daily lives. The fairly
comfortable farmer of Northern Italy and the poor *cafone* of the
South don't care about Mussolini's Empire. They want to be able
to sell their milk, their wheat and wine without being ridiculously
taxed and tied up with red tape; they want to be left in peace. They
have put up with harder work under fascism, they have put up with
privations and vexations, but they did not want to put on a uniform
and abandon their beloved fields to die with glory on foreign battlefields and they have resisted in their way by refusing to fight.

That is what the super-sophisticated minds of our Fleet Street
journalists or Ministry of Information officials are, of course, unable
to understand. They, who only know how to sell their pens to the
highest bidder, who have never defended anything but their cushy
jobs, sneer and abuse the Italian people who are not prepared to die

for the benefit of the Axis' glory or for the defence of desert land decorated with a few victory arches.

The French, who have not the Italian's reputation for cowardice retreated in front of the Germans at a speed which makes Caporetto and Guadalajara look like a walk over. Like the Italians the French had been demoralized by years of political corruption and dictatorship, and had not been given, like the Germans and the Russians, a militarist and nationalist training to make them willing tools in the hands of the government.

Reuter's correspondent in an interview with the *Manchester Guardian* said that the Italians wanted peace: "unless the peace looks uglier than the war, and Mussolini, of course, is doing his best (not without success) to make it look fiendishly ugly . . . " Mussolini is well assisted by British and American propaganda which has been pouring insults on the Italian people, condemning Mussolini while flattering Badoglio and the King, and spreading rumours about Mayor La Guardia coming to Europe to be made military dictator of Italy. The methods of intensive bombing used at Pantelleria and in many important cities do not offer prospects of a very bright future for the Italian people.

What is the antidote to Mussolini's propaganda? Some Italian anti-fascists are trying to form a Free Italy Legion, under the Garibaldi flag, which proposes to march into Italy with Allied troops. Bringing "liberty" at the point of bayonets, and having to defend themselves with British and American troops against the people they are going to unshackle!

The days are far distant when Britain, isolated, and on the brink of defeat, talked of revolution on the Continent. Having no planes, no arms, our democratic leaders were prepared to use socialist and revolutionary methods and slogans. Now that they are well provided with tanks, guns, fighters and American "fortresses" they forget about the armies of the French revolution and would more gladly model themselves on the hordes of Genghis-khan.

Their game is obvious now, but let us not forget how our socialists were fooled. Let us not forget, because from this there are some lessons to draw. Just as our democrats were prepared to consider revolutionary means when preparing their suitcases for Canada, they are now talking of an idealistic post-war Europe. Now, because

victory is not in their pockets yet. When and if it is, the "free determination of peoples" will spell armies of occupation in Italy, Germany, wherever it suits them; feeding the starving people of Europe,
will spell taxation to pay for the costs of war; free trade union movements will mean the crushing of any independent workers' movements,
and the pitiless extermination of any revolutionaries.

The Allied Governments have nothing to offer to the Italian
people. It will be for the British people to help them by themselves
getting rid of the future oppressors of Italy: the Churchills, Edens,
Morrisons, and all the rotten clique which rules us now.

June, 1943.

23. ONE YEAR OF STRUGGLE IN "LIBERATED" ITALY

SINCE THE fall of Mussolini on July 25th of last year no movement
has taken place in Europe which can be compared with the revolt
of the Italian people after the fall of the dictator. Not even the
opening of the Second Front has given rise to a wave of strikes such
as followed the collapse of the fascist régime in Italy.

The Italian people have shown that they did not expect freedom
to be brought to them at the point of Allied bayonets but believed in
conquering it themselves; by fighting the fascist police and officials
who had held them under their despotic rule; by occupying the
factories of the capitalists who had sheltered for twenty years under
the wing of Mussolini; by deserting from the army and sabotaging
the war industries.

Throughout August, 1943, in Milan, Rome, Turin, Bologna and
dozens of other towns the Italian workers declared general strikes and
fought in the streets. The revolutionary movement was so deep and
widespread that it was obvious that it would succeed in uprooting
fascism from Italy once for all. The Allies who had been talking
for three years of the need for revolution on the Continent did not,
however, greet with enthusiasm the revolutionary movements in Italy.
Far from it; Churchill talked with alarm of the danger of anarchy in
Italy and of being left with no responsible government to negotiate
with. Faced with a revolution which was not concocted in the offices

of the Ministry of Information or before the B.B.C. microphones, the
only thought of the American and British governments was to crush
it as soon as possible. Churchill had graduated in the art of counter-
revolution with his attempts to suppress the Russian revolution; he
was not able to send an expeditionary force to fight the Turin and
Milan workers but instead he sent heavy bombers to sow destruction
on the revolutionary industrial centres.

The delay of the Allies to conclude an armistice with Badoglio
can only be explained by their desire to quell any revolutionary up-
risings on Italian soil. For this purpose it was necessary to be able
to treat Italy as if she were still an enemy country. Though the Italian
people had given ample proof of their will to fight fascism, even with
their lives, they were treated as enemies; American, British and Italian
soldiers were left to kill one another in Sicily; the civilian population
in the North was butchered by Allied bombs. For six weeks from
July 25th to September 3rd the Allies carried on their counter-revolutionary measures while Germany was preparing to invade Italy. When
eventually the Allies decided to negotiate with the Government of
Badoglio they struck a final blow at the Italian masses. By recog-
nising Badoglio as the "liberator" of Italy they gave the people a new
master as hated and despised as Mussolini had been. The impudent
message that Churchill and Roosevelt sent to Badoglio on the 11th
September gave Badoglio and not the Italian people the credit for
having freed Italy from fascism:

"Marshal Badoglio, it has fallen to you in the hour of your country's agony to take the first decisive step to win peace and freedom
for the Italian people and to win back for Italy an honourable place
in the civilisation of Europe.
You have already freed your country from Fascist servitude.
There remains the ever more important task of cleansing the Italian
soil from the German invaders."

While Allied leaders sent complimentary messages to Badoglio
they were not so generous with the Italian masses, who merely got
bombed in the North and starved in the "liberated" South.

When Mussolini fell, the Italian people saw their task clearly;
they had to cleanse the country of all fascist institutions and set up
a new régime. Did the Allies help them in their task? On the con-

WAR *For Anarchism*
COMMENTARY

Vol. 5. No. 5.   JANUARY, 1944.   TWOPENCE

The Kharkov Trial

THE KHARKOV CIRCUS has ended and to the theatre applause of the assembled population and the lukewarm and doubtful approval of the British Press the German soldiers Wilhelm Langheld, Reinhardt Retzlav, Hans Ritz and the Russian lorry driver Michael Bulanov are hanged. We cannot tell, from the evidence revealed, whether or not the men are guilty as accused or if the alleged atrocities have been committed, but certain features of the play merit comment.

As in the celebrated "Moscow trials", the chief evidence is furnished by the accused themselves who confessed. In English law confession is doubtful evidence and we recall cases even of murder, where self-accused prisoners have been found not guilty. Even Russian law technically recognises the above sound principle, but in practice relies on its violation.

An equally dangerous innovation in judicial procedure is the Propaganda Trial, a trial which is staged not so much to discover guilt and award punishment or acquittal, but as an addition to the already extensive propaganda technique of governments. Looked at purely in a judicial sense a trial should be entirely free of propaganda. Judicially, the purpose of a trial is to discover the truth of the case. The purpose of propaganda is to sell an idea;

Adolf: "It isn't only *my* dustbin which stinks !"

WAR *For Anarchism*
COMMENTARY

Vol. 5, No. 10.   MID-MARCH, 1944   TWOPENCE

Strikes Everywhere

"It is sheer Anarchy", Will Lawther attacking the miners' strike in the Sunday Express *of March* 12, 1944.

SERVILE ADVOCATES OF the "war effort" would have us believe that strikes in war time are limited to Britain. Even the lying capitalist press is forced to admit the reverse, for through the fine mesh of press censorship filters news of class struggle the world over.

Most heavily censored has been news of the General Strike in Paraguay, South America. Yet from the few brief flashes from that country we learned last week that tens of thousands of workers were daily joining the strike; that transport and other workers were vigorously defending themselves against the police in the capital Asuncion and that railwaymen were tearing up the tracks to prevent the military using the railways.

In Australia the Labour politicians pass new repressive laws to prevent mining and other strikes and threaten the miners with military conscription if they dare to exercise the most elementary, the most fundamental right of Labour—the right to withdraw one's labour power.

In the U.S.A., workers, particularly miners, auto and aircraft workers, use the strike weapon to force up wages and render impotent the anti-labour legislation of the Roosevelt régime.

WAR COMMENTARY

For Anarchism

Vol. 5. No. 8.   MID-FEBRUARY, 1944   TWOPENCE

DOWN WITH FRANCO !

SPAIN HAS RECEIVED a great deal of attention from our journalists and politicians recently. During the past four years of war a discreet silence was kept about Franco and his régime. The daily shooting of anti-fascists, the prisons filled with revolutionaries, with women and children guilty only of having family connections with suspected elements, the suppression of every elementary liberty, were covered with an hypocritical veil.

The Press shed tears on Nazi atrocities, on imprisoned Frenchmen and starving Greek children, but not a word of sympathy has been found for the exhausted, starving, suppressed Spanish people. The

WAR *For Anarchism*
COMMENTARY

Vol. 5, No. 13.   MAY, 1944   TWOPENCE

UNDER THE AXE
OF BEVIN

IF DR. LEY and Herr Himmler came down by parachute to-day upon Whitehall, they would find very little unfamiliar except the architecture and the uniforms, and we can be sure they would be full of congratulations for the way in which their 'opposites', Messrs. Bevin and Morrison, are transforming Britain into a National Socialist State, and bringing the New Order here into line in every respect with that which exists on the continent.

For this May Day, when we celebrate the struggle of the workers throughout the world not only for the social revolution but also for the scanty benefits which they gained after bitter fights within the existing system, the workers find themselves subjected to an attack on the part of the Government which aims at the very foundations of their liberties, in that it attempts, by threatening the most barbarous penalties, to prevent the workers from making use of the sole weapon with which they can fight effectively either for better conditions under the present system or for the ending of that system and its replacement by a society which will not admit exploitation and authority.

This is the new Order under which it is laid down that 'No person shall declare, instigate or incite any

xii.

THE BOMBARDMENT OF LONDON

THE GOVERNMENT idiot who invented the term "beautiful bombs" must have felt a wave of æsthetic ecstasy sweep over him when the first of the German flying bombs struck London. The bombs are not only more devastating than the average bomb of previous raids on London, but the diabolical ingenuity of this invention arouses the imagination. Worst of all, the bombardment lasts, on and off, twenty-four hours a day, seven days a week.

Although the use of the new weapon by the Germans was anticipated by the Government, no preparation was made for the expected attack. New deep shelters, built a long while ago, give protection to less than one per cent. of the population of Greater London. Four years have passed since the first air raids on London, nearly five years since the war began and nearly six years since the war scare of the "Munich crisis", yet London still lacks sufficient surface shelters. It was possible to have completed enough deep shelters years ago. Instead we have had "London can take it" propaganda by persons who had retired to their country houses.

Nothing can dampen the cheerfulness of these optimists, an optimist being one who doesn't care what happens, so long as it doesn't happen to him. Scarcely less irritating than the whirr of the bombs in flight are the cheerful voices of the B.B.C., the apologia of Mr. Morrison and the press reports of the slight damage created by a ton of high explosive. I am almost kidded to expect one of these new weapons to explode and shower us with confetti, paper streamers and toy balloons after the manner of those fabulous bombs and shells "made in Czechoslovakia" we read of in the early war days. From Mr. Churchill's estimate of the casualties it seems that one of these bombs is no more dangerous than a drunken motorist driving his Rolls Royce "flat out" to provide himself a few hours amusement.

The Cry of the Vultures

Political kite hawks are quick to cash the present opportunity. In a London factory the Communists proposed a new warning system. The alert was to be sounded at the time of the outside sirens and the men and women continued work as at present. Then, if danger approached, the roof spotters sounded "imminent danger" but instead of going to the shelters as at present the workers continued their jobs. A third signal was proposed, a "crash signal", on hearing which the workers flopped on the floor or under bench or machine, for that meant the bomb was coming directly at the factory. Such a scheme carried out would mean a mass slaughter, not only by blast, but also from the glass, loose metal, scrap and tools which make a factory a death trap in aerial attack. Of course the shambles was to be organised in the name of the Second Front and all that.

What exposes the political character of this Communist showman's move is the well-known fact that aircraft and munition production is slack throughout the country and even the managements do not ask for such useless heroics. It is noteworthy that the meeting to discuss this scheme called by the Communist shop stewards during the lunch hour was abandoned three times because of the "imminent danger"

(Continued on p. 10)

Printed by Express Printers, 84a Whitechapel High St., London, E.1   Published by Freedom Press, 27 Belsize Road, London, N.W.6

WAR. *For Anarchism*

COMMENTARY.

Vol. 5, No. 21.   SEPTEMBER 1944   TWOPENCE

The Betrayal of Poland

AT DAWN ON September 1st, 1939, the German Army invaded Poland. On September 3rd, 1939, in execution of a pledge to guarantee the frontiers of Poland, Britain declared war on Germany. On this fifth anniversary, after five years of hard work and hard living, with Allied victory in sight, it is proper to review the progress made towards Polish independence. It is but a poor excuse to say, as do some of our opponents, that the Polish issue was but a pretext for the war, which would have been fought in any case. However considered, the issue of Polish independence was a major issue of the war—the issue chosen by the British Government. The stand against war we took in 1939 was opposed by Lefts, Socialists and Labourites of the *Tribune* and *Reynolds* type; it is proper to judge

them too by the same issue.

So far from safeguarding the frontiers of Poland, the war has brought out an even more bitter and potent enemy of Poland and swung some of the 1939 friends of Poland in this country into spiteful hatred of their one-time champion. Stalin's Russia, like the Russia of the Tsars, and the unprincipled "Russia, right or wrong" clique in this country, are set upon the destruction of the independent Polish nation. No better test of their sincerity could be taken than this issue. Their arguments and sincerity are less convincing than those of a vendor of quack medicine.

Russian-Polish Relations

After the Russian Revolution of 1917 the countries conquered by the Tsars took the opportunity to break

WAR COMMENTARY

For Anarchism

ol. 5, No. 22.　　　　MID-SEPTEMBER, 1944.　　　　TWOPENCE

WHAT'S COOKING?

DURING THE PAST fortnight a perceptible and even obtrusive change has taken place in the public mood towards the war and its conclusion. Events move so rapidly that it is difficult to realise that only a few days ago we were still living in an atmosphere of fear and uncertainty caused by the presence of the flying bomb attacks and what seemed the imminent probability of attacks from V2 and other hypothetical terror machines. Then the end of the war was discussed rather as a compensating possibility for present dangers than as a certainty.

Now, almost literally overnight, the whole mental scene has changed. The flying bombs are almost forgotten, except by those who suffered directly from their effects, and V2 has been relegated by most people into the realms of mythical fancy. The sweeping military successes of the allies, the apparent disintegration of the German army on the Western Front, have given rise to a general feeling of confidence that the war in Europe will be over soon, in a matter of weeks or possibly even days.

The recent actions of the Government show that they are willing to foster this idea of an imminent peace. The compulsory drills of the Home Guard have been abolished. Blackout is virtually to cease on the 17th September, and the hours of duty of firewatchers and voluntary Civil Defence workers are to be reduced to a mere fraction of what they are at present. Statements by political leaders and newspaper writers are all made in a tone of judicious confidence which is intended to impress the reader or listener.

We do not take upon ourselves the role of prophets,

WAR *For Anarchism*
COMMENTARY.

Vol. 5, No. 23. OCTOBER, 1944 TWOPENCE

THE GUILTY STAIN!

WARS ENTAIL ENDLESS sacrifice and suffering. They also involve disillusionment, for it soon becomes apparent that no positive gains emerge from all the bloodshed and cruelty. The last war "to make the world safe for democracy" enthroned dictatorships all over Europe, and the present war "to destroy militarism for ever" has succeeded in introducing peacetime conscription of the male population in England—the only European country which had so far stood out against this militarist measure. Nor do politicians hold out any hope of this being the last war. But in that case the sacrifices will have been made in vain, and people dare not face that reality. As in the last war, they are passionately determined that "it must never happen again", and a tremendous hatred for the causes of war is developing once more.

Victorious politicians are not slow to exploit this feeling, by raising the question of war guilt. If they can fix the responsibility for the horror of war on to the defeated enemy they hope to conceal the fundamental causes of war. For of course wars will continue so long as the profit motive compels national economics to "expand or burst", so long as the world is cursed by the competitive search for markets abroad with their finally inevitable armed conflicts.

In the context of capitalism, the conception of "war criminals" is really ludicrous. All the nations of the world are supposed to be driven into war by a handful of wicked politicians in the enemy countries. Even the Labour Party recognized the idiocy of this conception: Before 1939 they were never tired of pointing out that the policy of the National Government was

trary, they gave their support to Badoglio and the King who were both hated by the Italian people as Mussolini's tools; they demoralised and disorganised the population of the industrial centres by deliberate bombing; they crushed any attempt to set up a free régime in the South of Italy by handing over the administration of these countries to the reactionary rule of AMGOT (Allied Military Government of Occupied Territories).

One year has passed and the Allied governments have proved faithful to their initial policy of crushing revolutionary movements and giving their support to fascists who have made good by becoming Allied Quislings. The King, through pressure from Italian parties had to resign after the fall of Rome but the Monarchy remains. Prince Umberto can hardly be described as representing the aspirations of the Italian people and it may not be out of place to remind our Allies that it was he who led the Italian forces into Nice when Mussolini "stabbed France in the back". Perhaps it is too much to expect Mr. Churchill to mention in his next speech that when that stabbing, which he never fails to mention, was carried out, it was his co-belligerent, Umberto, who was carrying the knife.

Badoglio has had to go and who has replaced him but that old, compromised politician Bonomi. Bonomi was expelled from the Socialist Party in 1911 on account of his support for the Italian aggression in Lybia. When, after the first war, he was Minister of War in Giolitti's cabinet, Bonomi circularised all formations of the Italian Army with instructions to help the Fascist squads. Arms were given to the Fascist forces and Army officers joined them, thus greatly helping Mussolini to establish his reign of terror.

The fact that Communists figure in the Bonomi Government is far from reassuring. Togliatti, fresh from Moscow, can only be considered as a faithful tool of Stalin; Stalin who did not scruple to sign commercial treaties with Mussolini, to help him during the war against Abyssinia and to recognise his successor Badoglio (in Kharkov, minor German officials who were accused of having gassed Russians were hanged; for Italy, Badoglio who has gassed Abyssians is honoured). They give their loyal support to the Allied conquerors and prevent strikes of protest from taking place.

It is the tragedy of the Italian people that they have to fight not only against corrupt politicians and Allied reactionary administrators but also against the Communist Party which, exploiting the Russian victories and the myth of a Socialist Russia may, at least for a time gain considerable influence. Angelica Balabanoff, who was one of the most prominent members of the Italian Socialist Party sees this danger:

"Recessions as well as advances are to be expected (in Italy), not only because of the immeasurably difficult and tragic situation of the country now and during the aftermath of the war, but also because of the immediate menace: the bolshevik intervention in Italy, with its corruption, disintegration, intrigues and cynicism, political and physical terror and other despicable methods it connotes. The rehabilitation and salvation of the fascist monarchy by the Russian rulers is neither their first nor their last betrayal."

But she adds:

"Of one thing we can be sure: just as Fascism was incapable of subjugating the spirit of the Italian masses, so bolshevism will find that human dignity and class consciousness are stronger than demagogy, allurements, terror and money." (*The Call,* New York, 5/5/44).

The hope of the Italian people lies in the class consciousness and in the love of freedom they have displayed particularly after the fall of Mussolini and also in the deep-rooted distrust of governments and political parties. Foreign journalists have lamented the lack of interest of the Italians in the new government, in the fight between parties, and in Allied propaganda. They forget that the Italian people have been subjected for over twenty years to the most intense and all-pervading propaganda and have learned that the only way to keep their heads and not become mere robots is to shut their eyes and ears and try to work things out with their own plain commonsense. This explains how the Italian masses with practically no organisation were able to start a revolutionary movement which has not been surpassed since the beginning of this war. The French who had been under fascist rule for a much shorter period, who are apparently efficiently organised and provided with arms, are yet to rise as the Italians did.

The Italian workers may, in time, unite and co-ordinate their efforts and turn to a syndicalist organisation, based on factory and peasant committees, which alone can give them guarantees of freedom and independence. It will be the result not of political intrigues but of the spontaneous action of the workers. It will have nothing in common with the General Confederation of Labour (the Italian reformist Trade Union) which has been formed again in Rome by agreement between various parties and which groups communists and catholics alike.

The Italian anarchist paper *La Rivoluzione Libertaria* which first appeared in Bari at the end of June of this year stresses the need to organise with the maximum freedom and autonomy: "The only vital syndicalist organs are those born in the factories and in the fields, from below upwards, from the free will of association of the workers". Underground anarchist papers have also appeared in several towns of Northern Italy. It is to be hoped that their appeals to the Italian workers to get rid of their fascist masters and to refuse to accept new ones whether they call themselves liberals, democrats or communists, will be heard and that Italy will once again give birth to a strong anarchist and syndicalist movement.

On this anniversary of the fall of Fascism we are sending to our Italian comrades and to all true revolutionaries our fraternal greetings. We shall help them by intensifying the struggle here against capitalism and war; the revolution is indivisible and anarchists all over the world can all help the Italian revolution by their work for justice and freedom.

August, 1944.

24. ITALY TO-DAY—THE PRICE OF LIBERATION

ITALY HAS been liberated now for over a year and one would expect the blessings of Allied rule to have made themselves felt, yet all reports coming out of the country show that the conditions there are catastrophic. However, little interest is shown in Britain for the plight of the Italian people, partly because the English Press purposely avoids talking about the economic condition of Italy, partly because the reports of the food situation in France, Belgium and Greece monopolise people's interest by their dramatic nature.

This reticence of the Press and of the people responsible for the situation in Italy to-day is understandable as the record of one year of Allied occupation is a record of complete failure. The food situation is far worse than under Mussolini; political liberty granted to the Italian people is carefully limited as is shown by the new Press decrees. The Italian Government are puppets in the hands of the Allies who have the power to impose Badoglio or veto the appointment of Sforza as Foreign Minister. The administration of the country is still in the hands of corrupt fascist bureaucrats; new laws cannot be promulgated; purges cannot be started without A.M.G.'s consent; the Italian army is led by the same generals as under fascism; in Rome the people starve while the aristocracy entertains Allied leaders at sumptuous banquets.

The word starvation has been so extensively used since the beginning of the war that we all hear it with a certain callousness. China starves, India starves, Greece, Poland and Belgium are starving; that the Italian people should be starving as well seems merely in the order of things, fitting in the general pattern of war and occupation. This fatalistic attitude towards starvation is most revolting and pernicious. The famine in Italy, as the famine in India is a man-made famine which could easily be remedied if the people of the world were free to act in a natural and sensible way. Inflation and black-marketeering could be stamped out by the spontaneous action of the people if artificial rates of exchange were not fixed by the Government and if black-marketeers were not protected by the police. Shortage of food could be remedied by increasing production (this would be possible if the farmers and peasants were given some help instead of being submitted to forced requisitions) and by imports if the usual red herring—shortage of transport—was not brought up to prevent any action being taken.

Every man or woman should feel that starvation in other countries is his or her responsibility. It is with this in mind that we quote some of the heart-breaking descriptions of starvation in Italy. The Italian people need not pity but that practical steps should be taken to help them.

In *Life*, 19th June, 1944, a U.S. soldier describes the misery war has brought to the people of a small Sardinian town:

"We can't help thinking unwillingly we have helped bring this

degradation to Borgovecchio. We can't help feeling humble about
the appalling job of repairing and feeding and cleaning that faces
ue. We know that so far we have not done nearly enough of this job.

You catch the full impact of the town as soon as your vehicle
reaches the main square and is swallowed up by its mobs of children,
who run through the filthy streets like a restless swarm of minnows
in a muddy stream. They are everywhere—in your jeep, in your
pockets, in your hair. They are impudent little bandits who scarcely
seem like children.

What you see in their faces is clearly the imprint of war as if a
bullet had left its mark. So many of them are so unwashed, so
snotty-nosed, so sore-ridden, so drippy-eyed (with little droplets of
yesterday's hardened mucus clinging to the corners and lashes of their
eyes; with huge, open sores on their legs and arms where the flies
swarm unheeded) that when you do see a child with a well-scrubbed
face and the semblance of a clean garment you cannot help but
wonder how high up in the Fascist hierarchy his father had been in
order to wrest the precious soap."

Starvation is accompanied, as always, by a great increase in
prostitution. In the article quoted above the U.S. soldier describes
how:

"One boy of 9 years is the most persistent and the most successful too, judging from the groups of the G.I.s who engage him in
serious conversation and then follow him to the lower end of the
town where his sister, a prostitute, holds busy court. He has a
stump for a right arm, lost when our bombers blasted an important
coastal city; both his parents were killed at this time. He now spends
the entire day pimping about town for his sister and managing the
line of soldiers that forms outside her doorway."

This is not an isolated case; the *Manchester Guardian* correspondent reports an increase of prostitution in Rome and the anarchist
journal *Rivoluzione Libertaria*, published in Southern Italy, gives some
arresting facts as to the extent of child prostitution. In one hospital
in Naples alone, of 4,000 females infected by venereal diseases who
were examined over a period of a fortnight, about half of them were
under age. In that hospital there are girls contaminated and pregnant
who are 13, 12 and even ten and a half years old. A girl of twelve
had been admitted into a hospital suffering from injuries. She had

been beaten up by her father because she could not earn more than 2,000 lire per day whereas her fourteen year old sister earned from 4,000 to 5,000 lire.

It cannot be said that the Governments in this country and in America are unaware of the terrible conditions existing in Italy to-day. The report of the Trade Union delegation who visited Italy during the summer of this year gives the facts very plainly. After pointing out that people who have a job earn between 50 and 150 lire per day it goes on to say that "a very modest meal in a third-class restaurant costs between 100 and 200 lire. Olive oil (an important commodity for Italian feeding) costs 40 lire per litre when available and rationed. Black market prices range from 50 lire (Bari) to 550 lire (Rome)—a pair of leather shoes costs between 3,500 and 4,500 lire— any basis for social life of the population is lacking. The result is corruption, looting and black-market activities on a large scale, or starvation." What are the Trade Unions doing about these appalling conditions? They have a member in the cabinet, they have members in the House. Have they registered any protest? As was to be expected the leaders have done nothing but the rank and file have done nothing either; not a single demonstration, not a meeting of protest has been organised. This must be said to the shame of the British working class.

The declaration by President Roosevelt and Mr. Churchill issued on the 26th September and which was interpreted as an "encouragement for Italy" does not mention the terrible conditions under which the Italians are living, but envisages reconstruction of an Italian economy. This is not for humanitarian reasons but so that Italy can play a more active part in the war against Germany. The declaration says: For military reasons we should assist the Italians in restoration of such power systems, their railways, motor transport, roads and other communications, as enter into the war situation, and for a short time send engineers, technicians, and industrial experts into Italy to help them in their own rehabilitation". Instead of devising means by which Italy can recover from the sufferings of war Allied statesmen only think of new ways of bringing her into the war again.

U.N.R.R.A. has finally decided to send medical aid and other essential supplies to Italy. The United States member of U.N.R.R.A.

Administration Council at their conference in Ottawa recommended
that help should be given to Italy partly for military reasons, partly
because Italy was a Catholic country.   This 'humanitarian" said:

"It was not a question of coddling the Italian people but to see
that the populations are put into a state of repose behind the Army.
The infant mortality in Rome is now 50%.   Every tenth man or
woman you pass in the street in Rome will be a corpse before the end
of the year.   He reminded the Council that Italy was the centre of
the Catholic world.   Should U.N.R.R.A. express a lack of interest
this fact would be communicated far and wide to persons in occupied
areas and throughout the world."

If Rome had been the centre of the Moslem or Buddhist world
U.N.R.R.A. presumably would not have felt compelled to help its
inhabitants!

*   *   *

In a country where people starve there never is any freedom
of the Press as the Government has to take every possible step to
suppress popular criticisms and unrest.   Officially the freedom of the
Press has been reintroduced in Italy but in fact the decrees governing
the Press which have become effective as from the 1st August, 1944,
give power to prevent or to suppress any publication, to the Prefetti
(heads of the administration in a department) and to a Commission
composed of officials, most of whom were appointed during the fascist
régime.

The decree states that whoever wants to issue any publication,
even if it is not a periodical, must obtain permission from the Administration of the Department (prefettura).

Any change of owners, editors or administrators, political line
or aim of the publication must be notified to the Commission through
the same channels.

In conclusion the decree states that political censorship is abolished, only military censorship being retained.   We certainly would
not have guessed it from the text of the decree!   One must remember
that the Prefetti in Italy had been appointed by Mussolini; that most
of them still remain in power and that the officials and priests who
compose the Commission were also the tools of the fascist régime.
Of course these people cannot openly express their fascist view any

longer and are obliged to allow the publication of socialist, communist and anarchist publications but it is not unreasonable to fear that they will exert their reactionary influence whenever they have an opportunity.

One hears quite a lot about the changes which have taken place in the administration of 'liberated" countries but one must treat with the greatest suspicion the news that new Commissions and Liberation Committees have been set up. These are more often than not the old fascist institutions baptized with a new name. One must remember that any change must be first okayed by A.M.G. and the Italian Government (with the King's son at its head); that it is the leaders at the top who nominate them and that therefore those new institutions cannot claim to represent the wishes of the masses.

An example of this ineffective whitewashing in the administration concerns the very important problem of grain collection. The American *Daily Worker* pompously announced on 20th May, 1944:

"Fausto Gullo, the new minister of agriculture, and a Communist, is now putting a remarkable grain collection into practice. It is going to undermine the whole social basis of fascism, and—what is more— will soon relieve the Allies of any need to send wheat to Italy."

Unfortunately for the *Daily Worker* the Office of War Information Bulletin (10/5/44) published a detailed account of Gullo's scheme which far from justified the boosting given to it by the *Daily Worker*. This O.W.I. report is quoted in *The Call* (14/7/44) with appropriate comments which we cannot do better than quote extensively:

"The fact is that under Mussolini's fascism, the 'People's Granaries' existed under the name of 'Ammassi' (wheat collection). The Communist paper's report indicates that changing its name will 'undermine the whole social basis of fascism'! But the 'people' have as little to do with the 'granaries' as they had to do with the 'ammassi', which were controlled entirely by Mussolini's non-elected government. These 'three thousand village committees' of Gullo's are just as undemocratic.

The O.W.I. Bulletin of May 10, which evidently was used by the *Daily Worker* in order to mislead its readers, reported that Gullo had ordered such 'advisory' committees (they are not even action committees!) for the collection and the distribution of wheat and barley to consist of eight members, with the mayor of the town, as chairman, to appoint the other seven.

Two members are to be farmers representing the landowners; two are to represent the agricultural workers; another member will be nominated by the (Catholic) Bishop; another will be the chief of the local carabinieri (royal police); and one will be the local chief of the administration of the Department of Agriculture, who will act as secretary."

Now let us look at this picture: No Italian town has an elected mayor. Every community, large or small, is ruled by a government appointee, whether under Mussolini, Badoglio or Bonomi. These appointees in the great majority of cases are still Fascist or pro-Fascist, as American Press correspondents have so often pointed out.

The carabinieri have been under Mussolini's orders for more than twenty years. Only the good (according to Fascist standards) elements were admitted to this corps by Mussolini and only the 'very good" were promoted. The chief of the carabinieri was very good.

Mr. Gullo, having "communistically" decided to project the clergy into such temporal matters as grain distribution, did not pick on the local priest, who has not always been pro-Fascist, but decided instead to have someone picked by the Bishop. As is well known, the Italian high clergy has been boldly pro-Fascist. In pre-Fascist Italy the representatives of the clergy and police were never called upon to take any part in the civil administration of the country!

How anti-Fascist the "representatives of the landlords" are will be understood by recollecting that the landlords were the first organizers and financial supporters of the "squadre d'azione" (Italian edition of the Nazi storm troopers) whose aim was physical destruction of the agricultural workers Union and the peasant co-operatives and the murdering of Labour militants.

But "representatives" of the agricultural workers also are included—two out of eight. Don't let that fool anybody. As the O.W.I. Bulletin clearly states, these are merely two persons (not necessarily farm workers) nominated by the appointed mayor to "represent" the agricultural workers. Their "representation" will be as "anti-Fascist" as the "mayor" who appoints them.

An A.M.G. officer in Naples said to the American journalist

F. C. Painton: "We said we came as liberators, but failure to meet obvious food shortages is not an act of liberation . . . If we do elsewhere in Europe what we are doing in Italy, then the peace is lost before the war is won." This is the opinion of an Allied official; as far as the Italian people are concerned their war has been lost long ago, when the fall of Mussolini simply meant a change of masters for them. The only hope is that the mood of despair and cynicism which made Italians write on the walls "Down with everybody" will change to one of self-reliance and resolution to bring about a radical change in the economical and political conditions of the country.

December, 1944.

25. SAVE THE GERMAN PEOPLE

ONE CANNOT accuse the Allies of a lack of foresight regarding the future of the German people. Newspapers report that already graves are being dug in anticipation of the high mortality due to starvation which will occur this winter. How often have we heard during the last few years of the Nazi atrocity which consisted of making people dig their own graves in concentration camps! The Allies are not fascist brutes; they are merely "realists" who, knowing that the people they starve will be too weak this winter to bury their dead and to dig their own graves then, want the job done three or four months beforehand.

The famine in Germany, like all the famines which have taken place in Europe and Asia during the past century, is a man-made famine, due not to actual shortage of food but to political factors. The partition of Germany into different zones of occupation and the displacement of millions of people as well as the systematic looting carried out by the occupation forces are the main causes of starvation.

Only a few weeks ago at Potsdam the Allies declared that populations would be transported only if it could be done in "a humane and orderly fashion". What happened in fact is that in Berlin and the Eastern provinces there are between ten and twelve million people who have been expelled without food or clothes from their homes in the Sudetenland, Eastern Germany and East Prussia. These refugees, mostly women and children, are dying on the way in large numbers, alongside the railways and on roads, and those who reach their destination find a total lack of food and housing accommodation.

Another of the Potsdam promises which was never kept was that Germany would remain an economic unit. Instead, the Russians, French, British and Americans each pursue their own policy. The great Eastern producing belt has been cut off from the rest and this makes it impossible for Germany to feed all the refugees who are streaming into the country. There seems to be little co-operation between the occupying powers; people are sent from one region to another without information being previously exchanged as to the conditions they will find there. The Russians are complete masters of the zone they occupy and they do not allow journalists to find out what is going on. British planes are not even permitted to fly over Russian occupied territory.

Captain Raymond Blackburn, Labour M.P. back from a tour of the British Occupation zone in Germany writes in the *News of the World,* 16/9/45:

"It would appear that the Russians have killed or deported to the East most of the cattle. They have dismantled much of the factory equipment and transported it to the East. They have even taken up the railway lines in places and thereby decreased the flow of food and other goods through the narrow lifeline that connects Berlin with Western Germany."

This compares badly with Stalin's reasoned statement in his Order of the Day of the 23rd February, 1942:

"Sometimes the foreign Press engaged in prattle to the effect that the Red Army's aim is to exterminate the German people and destroy the German State. This, of course, is a stupid lie, and a senseless slander on the Red Army. The Red Army has not and cannot have any such idiotic aims."

Not only are the Russians carrying on the "Idiotic aims" of extermination, but they encourage the same policy in countries they occupy. Moscow-controlled Warsaw radio describes the process of Polish "settlement" in the seized districts of Eastern Germany— Silesia, Pomerania, Mazuria. The Polish "settlers" go to Germany not to settle there but to loot and return to Poland laden with all kinds of goods.

The broadcast, quoted in the *Manchester Guardian* (13/9/45) condemned the looting not out of decency to the German people but because it was not done under proper authority. The Germans looted Poland; Germany should be looted in return, but:

"Strong measures were needed, since the professional 'gleaners' are (1) stealing from the State by travelling free; (2) overcrowding the trains; (3) falsifying statistics of the settlement movement to the West because the most expert statistician could not guess which are the real and which the false settlers; (4) denuding the areas so completely that the real settlers find emptiness."

The *Daily Worker* will go on denouncing the looting of a few shops by Polish workers in Germany, when looting is tolerated and even encouraged by the Russians in the area of Germany they control.

Against this background of starvation and pestilence the question of re-educating the German people appears like a sinister jest. University professors might be hired to write highly intellectual articles on what the Germans should read and think; the B.B.C. may broadcast highbrow programmes on English literature; expurgated schoolbooks may be printed, but what is the good of all this to a starving population?

It is doubtful if German children will get any education at all, let alone re-education. A few schools have re-opened; they have no windows, no heating, no books (plans are for one book for ten pupils and that is nowhere near being reached yet).

J. B. Priestley during his visit to Germany was particularly struck by the plight of the children:

"What I have seen and heard from responsible relief workers on the spot shocks the conscience—and it would upset the conscience of anyone in England could they visit Berlin and see for themselves.

These children are guiltless—yet they are the ones who are paying the heaviest part of the price for Germany's guilt. They are blameless on all counts. Yet their suffering is the greatest. I believe that if the people of England could see the privations these children are exposed to there would be many who would willingly give up part of their rations, however small they may be, this winter."

This is the only practical suggestion that has been made so far, and the Save Europe Now committee, sponsored by V. Gollancz, the Bishop of Chichester, and Bertrand Russell, among others, has undertaken to collect names of people who would be willing to give up part of their rations to feed starving people on the Continent.

Among all the feelings of contempt, hatred and revenge which are expressed against the German people, these proposals come as a breath of sanity and an an example of real solidarity. But is it necessary to cut down the rations of the already often undernourished British worker in order to feed Europe?

Could not food be brought from North and South America where there is an over-abundance of it? Could not Denmark export food to Germany? An article in *The Leader*, 14/9/45 describes Danish shops as being full of bacon, eggs, butter and milk.

"Danes complain about the shortage of coffee and the glut of foods rationed in England. 'Why will you not buy our butter and eggs?' a Copenhagen housewife said, 'For my husband and daughter I cook fifty eggs a month'."

Food is there, lorries are lying idle, ships are being released from war purposes. What is needed is the will on the part of the British and American workers to help their German brothers. The example of the Swiss Trade Unions which have sent considerable quantities of food to Germany should be followed. Through agitation in the factories, in the co-operatives, the workers of this country could oblige the Government to send immediate help to Germany. A Labour Government will be responsible for thousands of deaths this winter, but the responsibility lies not only with the government but also with the apathy of the British workers, who must act before it is too late.

September, 1945.

26. In Darkest Germany

DURING RECENT years one's mind has been so saturated by accounts of atrocities, war massacres and famines, that one's powers of indignation, sensibility and anger have been considerably blunted. One feels so powerless against the accumulated lunacy of the whole world that one is tempted to look at it with an almost fatalistic eye. But reading a book like Victor Gollancz's *In Darkest Germany* shakes one with disgust and rage.

This book deals with the author's visit to the British Zone, and therefore the flimsy excuse that "it is no concern of ours" cannot be brought forward. It deals with conditions existing not in far-away India or China, not behind the well-guarded frontiers of Russia but on the other side of the North Sea, right under our noses.

The material contained in this book is not entirely new; part of the information has been published in various newspapers. But the mass of information is greater than can be found anywhere else and has been carefully checked by the author during his six weeks' visit to the British Zone. This, Gollancz believes, is the longest visit paid to the zone since "victory". Mr. Hynd, who is Chancellor of the Duchy, and Minister responsible for the British Zone in Germany, has not spent more than twenty-eight days in Germany during the past twelve months.

That a Socialist Government should be responsible for the conditions existing in the British zone is a tragic irony. You need all the hypocrisy and callousness of our politicians to deny that millions of people in Germany to-day are starving.

In Hamburg 100,000 people are suffering from hunger oedema or the equivalent, and in Regierungsbezirk Dusseldorf 13,000 people were being treated for this illness during the month of September (the number will be much greater during the winter). Active lung tuberculosis in Hamburg is at least five times as prevalent as before the war.

"All this doesn't mean," says Gollancz, "that people are dropping dead in the streets . . . The point is that a very great number of people feel wretchedly weak and ill, and that the health of the population as a whole is being undermined with such startling rapidity that, unless radical measures are taken to effect an improvement, the toll in one, two or three years' time will be appalling. It must be remembered that mortality from tuberculosis did not reach its climax until five years after the last war.

The Government has been carefully hiding behind the myth of the calories ration distributed to the German people. When Mr. Hynd declares in the House of Commons that the Germans are getting 1,550 calories, everybody feels satisfied.

The point is, as Gollancz abundantly proves in his book, that people were getting 8,500 grammes of bread instead of the full ration of 10,000 in 28 days. The cereal ration was not distributed so that the 1,548 calories were already reduced to 1,206. In other places he found that only 65 and 50% of the ration was obtainable. The same applied to skimmed milk. In the whole North Rhine region the deficiency since October 14th had been about 50%.

It is quite clear that in many cases the number of calories received is in fact a third less than on paper.

If lack of food undermines the health of the nation the absence of consumer goods, and in particular shoes and clothes, has also terrible consequences. In the schools he visited Mr. Gollancz found a large proportion of children with completely ruined shoes, and in their homes many people were going about bare footed. The official figure of the number of children's shoes needed for the period from July to December was, at the very minimum 6,200,000 but the total number of coupons issued for their purchase from May to December was 1,771,000.

Napkins, baby clothes, overcoats, blankets, mattresses are almost impossible to find. The children are the worst victims but it will not prevent people from justifying the inhuman treatment of the German people by saying: "They've brought it on themselves."

Several chapters of the book and a large number of photographs give a terrible picture of the housing conditions. Out of the 23 million Germans in the British zone several millions live in the atrocious conditions Gollancz describes, many more live in reasonably decent rooms but badly overcrowded. In Dusseldorf the average living space per person is 3.2 square metres, but there are still people living in extremely comfortable establishments and when Gollancz spent a night in a particularly damaged city his bedroom measured 720 square feet.

The demands for sending more food to Germany are met with

the excuse of world shortage, but what explanation can the Government give to the senseless destruction which is still carried out at the present time? The application of the Potsdam agreement, which is supposed to prevent a rebirth of the German military machine, plunges the German people still further into ruin.

Fertilizer factories are being destroyed when German agriculture needs them most urgently, and so are factories producing soda which would be a first necessity in a country where soap is a rare commodity. Cement factories are being closed down, though, as Gollancz remarks, cement can be used not only to build Siegfried Lines, but also to repair houses and to build new ones.

Kiel harbour is scheduled for destruction. If this is carried out it will be impossible to build up a whole series of light industries and the resultant unemployment has been estimated at 150,000 out of a population of 250,000.

Thirteen fishing vessels were blown up at Bremerhaven because they had been used as mine layers. They could have been reconverted into fishing boats and used to help alleviate the food position, but because of some lunatic agreement the fish had to remain in the sea and the people had to starve.

The irresponsible policy of the Allies in Germany is not calculated to impress the people with the advantages of democracy. Neither is the behaviour and mode of life of the occupying troops. Unnecessary vexations are meted out daily by British officials to German civilians, irrespective of whether they have always been anti-nazi or not.

The military character of the occupation is displayed everywhere in arrogant fashion. "The result of it all," says Gollancz, "is that when German liberals talk to German youth about militarism, the reply is—'But British militarism is just as bad'."

The British occupying forces behave like the master race. They eat well, they have plenty of cigarettes and drinks, German houses have been requisitioned to house them and German men and women employed to serve them. Labour and materials are freely spent on repairing clubs for British troops and in Hamburg 14,226 labourers were engaged in building a Garden City to house the Control Commission.

The "re-education" of the German people is hampered still

further by the totalitarian attitude adopted by the Allies towards the de-nazification of books. The Control Council Order of 13th May, 1946, prohibits the circulation not merely of books "supporting militarism, nationalism, and racialism" but also those "containing propaganda directed against the United Nations". As far as new books are concerned publishers are instructed that they are responsible that the works published "shall not include anything which reflects adversely upon . . . any of the Allied Powers".

Gollancz's book is a damning indictment of the policy of the British Government in Germany. The information it contains should be as widely known as possible and one cannot look at the photographs which illustrate the book without a feeling of shame and of revolt.

February, 1947.

27. GERMANY: MISERY AND CORRUPTION

MUCH HAS been said in Parliament and in the Press recently which confirms the statements Victor Gollancz makes in his book *In Darkest Germany.*

Mr. Hynd's optimistic declarations on the situation in the British zone have been challenged in the House and have been disproved by newspaper correspondents. The Anglo-American bi-zonal food programmes, introduced in January to achieve a common ration scale in the northern and southern provinces has not improved the conditions of the 23 million inhabitants in the British zone. Promises of a bigger meat ration have not been implemented and it is officially admitted that the 1,550 calories ration scale exists only on paper.

With the news of the grave food situation in Germany, of deaths from cold and 200 suicides in Berlin, of 7,233 people being arrested by the railway police in Hamburg for coal thefts during January, has also come the news of vast black market dealings by Allied troops in Germany.

The "merry game" of speculation in marks by British troops in Germany will cost the British taxpayer £20,000,000. Mr. Bellinger, Secretary of War, explained to the House that this sum was required to meet a loss in surplus marks and schillings in Germany and Austria. B.A.O.R. men bought cigarettes and other goods in Army canteens and sold them to civilians at enormously inflated prices. They used this money to buy other goods at the canteens, or to buy Savings Certificates and make deposits with the Post Office Savings Bank.

To have an idea of the profits made by some of the Allied troops one must remember that the cigarette ration to British troops and Control Commission staffs was, up to a few days ago, of 200 per week. Black market prices stood for months at four marks or two shillings a cigarette and even more. If he sold the whole of his ration the British soldier or official could make over two pounds a day. But it is often found more profitable to exchange cigarettes for cameras, electric fires, books, records, watches, jewels, and other goods.

Fortunes have been made in speculation and black market sales and in many cases large properties have been purchased by British personnel to invest these huge profits.

It is probably quite true that, as Mr. Bellenger has pointed out in self-defence, Britain was the first country to try to put a brake on black market transactions. But it gives one little hope as to the effects of occupation in Germany to know that American investigators estimate that illegal deals have so far cost the American Treasury not less than £250,000,000.

One gets a fairly good idea of the efficiency with which the American black market is organised from the advertisements which cover the continental editions of American newspapers.

To take one example: The Paris edition of the New York *Herald Tribune* contains over a dozen big advertisements by American firms offering A.P.O. personnel everything from duty free cigarettes to nylons, coffee, vegetable fat, chocolate, lipsticks, lengths of tweed (blue, grey, brown).

The American Star Trading Co. offers 2,000 cigarettes for $9.50 or £2 7s. 6d. If each cigarette is sold at 4 marks it will bring in 8,000 marks or, at the official rate, £200.

The American Overseas Shippers, Inc., N.Y., offers to ship by air mail 6 pairs of nylons for 13 dollars or 10lb. of the finest coffee and 7½lbs. of pure vegetable fat for 16 dollars.

Fraser, Morris & Co., Inc., claim to be "the originators of duty-free cigarettes! The idea that saved servicemen millions of dollars" and to have shipped 3,500,000 parcels in the past few years.

Now it is quite obvious that A.P.O. personnel receiving 200 cigarettes a week, well fed and looked after, receiving decent pay would hardly need thousands of cigarettes, coffee and cooking fats for their personal use. It can be argued that he wants these things as presents for friends and this may well happen in some cases but one can imagine what vast black market transactions are taking place when goods are supplied to the black marketeers by airmail, insured and at a low cost—without forgetting the legality of the whole transaction.

The presence of Allied wives and families in Germany has only worsened the morale of the occupation and it is not surprising that women are now being discouraged from going to Germany and even stopped altogether in the case of Hamburg. This is how the *News Chronicle* correspondent, S. L. Solon (31/1/47), describes the behaviour of Allied wives who were supposed to show the Germans the meaning of democracy in everyday life:

"The Allied wives have not failed to see the opportunity for easy plunder and the advantages of German coolie labour. Established on a caste system reflecting the ranks and positions held by their husbands, the women have each built up their little kingdoms where they command from one (on the lowest level) to a dozen or more servants.

The women with more leisure and fewer scruples have bounded merrily into the black market. The scramble for antiques, jewels, furs, furniture bought with 'cigarette marks' is the chief occupation of hundreds of them."

All the solutions of the German problem which have been put forward fail to give enough importance to these facts. The Allies are the conquerors and it is useless to ask them to behave otherwise. They behave as such in a small way by exchanging their cigarettes for cameras; that is the bottom of the ladder. At the top they steal raw material, factories and manufactured goods under cover of reparations. But the principle is the same—the weak have to accept the rule of the strong.

It is for this reason that the suggestions put forward by well-meaning people like Gollancz appear unrealistic. He accepts military occupation but he would like this occupation to be humane ("feed the Germans"), democratic ("stop behaving like inefficient totalitarians"), liberal and Christian.

This would only be possible if the countries occupying Germany to-day were not capitalist, totalitarian, imperialist powers. It is not an accident that the machinery of control is inefficient, cruel and corrupt. It merely reflects the spirit of the governments they represent—governments which prefer to destroy food rather than feed it to the German people—governments which ruthlessly destroy factories when workers cry out for work—governments which prefer to deal with docile Nazis rather than allow honest anti-fascists freedom to speak and write.

As long as the fate of Germany remains in the hands of the British, American and Russian governments, she will know misery and reaction. She can only expect solidarity from workers in other countries. Is the spirit of *Kameradschaft* completely dead? If hands can be stretched across frontiers when the lives of a few men are in danger why aren't they when millions of people are sinking into hopeless misery?

March, 1947.

28. FAMINE IN ROUMANIA

ACCORDING TO recent reports, the great Ukrainian famine has been followed by an equally disastrous one in Roumania as a result of the same drought, which affected the Moldavian plain almost as badly as it struck South Russia. This is the second drought which the Moldavian peasants have suffered in two years, and they are now near the end of their resources—many of them have actually reached the end.

The situation, bad in itself, has been aggravated by many avoidable circumstances. The devastation of the recent war has played its part in disrupting the carrying on of supply services in the country, but much more crippling circumstances have been the continued presence of a large Russian army, which, as elsewhere, lives parasitically on the land and has taken first priority on all crops, and the lack of any co-ordination in distribution—the black market in Bucharest is one of the most widespread and highly organised in Europe. But there has been little effort made by the Communist-controlled government to organise efficient supply services for the country areas. The result is that, while the rich in the capital are living as well as they live in any other European capital, the conditions of the poor in the famine areas are so bad that, according to a *Manchester Guardian* report:

" . . . the peasants are moving away in gangs in search of food, meanwhile eating grass and acorns and even chewing clay-bearing soil to assuage their hunger. They have slaughtered their cattle or bartered it for grain, and have even, it is said, consumed seed corn although the authorities soaked it in oil before distributing it."

To meet this situation, the measures taken by the Roumanian government are, even in the words of one of the well-censored Bucharest newspapers, "of symbolic rather than of effective value". Some children have been transferred to areas not affected by the famine, but very little in the way of supplies has been sent. Nor has there been any great display of international solidarity. Some of the neighbouring countries have sent small supplies of grain, but the authorities still estimate that there is a need for 50,000 wagons of grain in March alone. So far none of the great democratic powers has come forward to give any substantial help for the starving Roumanians.

Nor is the future likely to show any great and immediate improvement. Owing to disruption by war and political strife, it is officially estimated that the quantity of winter sowings this year is little more than half of last year. Further improvement will of course be hindered by the effects of the slaughter of cattle and destruction of seed grain during the present famine.

One cannot blame the Roumanian or the Russian governments for the drought. But one can blame them for the way in which they have allowed the peasants to be pillaged to feed their armies and for black market purposes, and have failed completely to provide any system that would prevent such a crisis. A social system based on efficient and voluntary mutual aid would undoubtedly have proved much more elastic in crises of this kind than the inefficient governmental system of coercion and class interest.

March, 1947.

3

United Nations

29. HORRORS OF THE PEACE

WITH THE end of 1945 it is time to take stock, and consider the larger issues involved in the transition from war to peace from the standpoint of the workers. First, the nearest home, so to speak, is the question of wages. Just as the war provided employment in a way that the peacetime years had wholly failed to do, so the prospect of unemployment once again returns with the peace. And whereas the labour shortage which existed under war economy caused wages to go up, whether from an increase in working time, through overtime, or more rarely, from an increase in wage rates, so the slackened demand for labour now means loss of overtime and so reduced total wages; or the peacetime increase of the cost of living offsets even further any war-time gains as to rates of pay; or frank unemployment threatens the workers' economic position. Thus a direct result of peace has been increased industrial unrest expressed through the major strikes in the past few months. But now some of the factors in the wage struggle are becoming more obvious. During the war, employers needed workers, and strikes were a serious threat to them, so they represented strikes as unpatriotic, and war-work as a necessity of the community which must not be interfered with. Now that such moral blackmail no longer applies, the lessened demand for labour also makes strikes less of a threat to employers, and therefore less powerful weapons in the hands of the workers. Thus the end of the war, considered from a purely economic angle, provides ground for disillusionment. And this feeling is still further enhanced by the continued behaviour of the Trade Union officials as agents of the

State for keeping "recalcitrant" workers in order—by defeating or cutting down demands for pay increases to meet the new situation.

But 1945 was also a year of profound disillusionment from a political point of view. It began amid the repression of Greek workers by British units under General Scobie. That conflict was brought to an end by agreements between E.A.M. leaders, the Greek Right, and the British authorities, whereby no reprisals were to be exacted and an amnesty for all prisoners of the civil war to be effected. On such assurances the Greek workers allowed themselves to be disarmed. But in fact full amnesty has never been granted, thousands remaining in prison even now. And the time has been used by the Greek Government to institute police measures to prevent any further demonstrations of popular resentment. Bevin, who specifically defended the Churchill cabinet's policy in Athens, has shown no concern to see that the conditions of last January's truce are put into force.

Similarly, many who saw in the Labour Party's access to power a hope of a less reactionary turn in foreign policy have been disillusioned by the failure to change the Conservative Government's attitude to General Franco. The shameful treatment meted out to Spanish anti-Fascist refugees, held as prisoners of war at Chorley, Lancs., provides another example ill-calculated to inspire hope for the future as a result of "victory". And now there are Indonesia and Indo-China as well.

Nor are the horrors of war dispelled with the peace. Winston Churchill, in 1943, held out to the peoples of occupied Europe hopes which liberation has scarcely confirmed. He declared that with the lifting of the Nazi yoke, the populations would once again receive adequate food and again enjoy freedom. Neither of these promises has been even approximately fulfilled. Every liberated country has felt a worsening of the food situation since the Allied liberation. Everywhere repressive laws are still in existence, and "freedom" quite illusory. And the plight of the defeated countries is such as to invite unfavourable comparisons by their peoples, between the Nazis and the new "freedom-loving" rulers, which are hardly conducive to feelings of optimism or hope about the future, but rather tend to deepen the apathy which helped the original imposition of totalitarian rule.

Animosity towards Fascist leaders is natural. But the trials of war criminals by the Allies have done much to create sympathy with these people. In particular the trials of Pétain and Laval in France, where ex-Vichy judges and prosecutors thundered against their former masters, provided an odious display of capitalist "justice". Many people in this country have been shocked at the State's evident determination to secure a conviction against such minor figures as Joyce and Amery, by having recourse to the 600 year old Treason Act of 1351. Many who formerly retained some respect for the law will have been disillusioned by these vindictive propaganda exhibitions, these ready concessions on the part of the State to what they believe to be the popular demand for scapegoats—scapegoats, however, who conveniently distract attention from people whose responsibility for the war is far heavier.

The moral corruption in our society which the unfulfilled promises of the war has brought to the notice of even the politically naïve, also appears in scientists who, like Pontius Pilate, wash their hands of the responsibilities which the atom bomb lays upon its producers. How feeble, how unconvincing, is all this talk about "controlling" the potentialities of atomic energy! Throughout history, the potential good which advances in knowledge have placed in men's hands, has almost always been vitiated by their actual use in the service of the ruling groups in society. And so it will be with the atom bomb. Fears about the future will not be allayed by the pious resolutions and political shifts. Treaties about atom bombs are not likely to be given any more respectful attention than the other scraps of paper which have decorated political history.

It is time scientists faced up to their responsibilities in such matters. If they groan at the cruel desolations their ingenuity has inflicted on suffering millions, then let them refuse to put their brains and their labour at the service of the political power groups which seldom use science to better the lot of the workers, but never hesitate to turn it to their own ends in wars.

And the workers who operate the factories which produce the atom bombs? Shall they stand by and say it is no concern of theirs? If Spanish workers could refuse to build prisons; if the anarchist syndicalist workers at Erfurt in Germany after the first world war could go on strike for months, refusing to make munitions, and preferring to see their jobs taken from them by reformist trade unionists rather than give in; if Australian dockers can refuse to load material for use against the Indonesians in the present far-Eastern struggle; if workers have made a stand on these issues in the past, cannot the British and American and Russian workers refuse to be a party to making atom bombs? If they did so refuse, would they not receive the approval of all those over whose lives the atom bomb has cast a new menacing shadow?

The same antithesis lies at the root of all the disillusion which the war has brought. Everywhere we see resources opened up, new possibilities for the realisation of material happiness. And at the same time, we see everywhere increasing misery, increasingly sordid results from the sacrifice of human life and idealism. 1945 has underlined this process, but it is never far beneath the surface of our society.

But as sordid events succeed one another it becomes increasingly clear that it is the class-divided society, the domination of the State over human individuals, which ensures that every advance in knowledge or technique is used for the benefit, not of mankind as a whole, but of the power interests of ruling minorities. This process becomes more and more evident with each meeting of politicians from the powerful States. When it is fully understood, and men act on this knowledge, then will the fruits of science and the accumulated experience of workers be placed at the service of society as a whole. If the pain and disillusionment of 1946 have their part in achieving these ends, they will not have been wholly in vain.

January, 1946.

30. British Intervention in Asia

Our War Minister, Mr. J. J. Lawson chose the moment when British marines, soldiers and airmen were shooting down the people of Southern Asia to pay this tribute to the British soldier:

"It has been said that the British soldier is the best ambassador we have. I think he is better than most ambassadors.

By the peculiar nature of his tasks, the British soldier is in some directions a genius. He has certain gifts of his own.

He always seemed to make people laugh. I have never known
an ambassador who could make people laugh."

The soldiers of the Labour Government of Britain are not
ambassadors of laughter. Java is bombed by rocket-firing Mosquitoes
and troops are concentrated at key points "ready for anything".
Indo-China is submitted to military rule; Indian demonstrators are
fired upon.

The man directing Britain's foreign policy, Ernest Bevin, who
declared at the Conference of the Labour Party in 1939: "I am
anxious to prevent the Labour Movement fighting for the preservation
of the Paris Bourse, the London Stock Exchange, and Wall Street",
is not only asking British soldiers to die to defend the interests of
those Big Three, but also to defend Dutch interests in Indonesia.

Let us remember once again the Big Lie, the principle of the
Atlantic Charter, which says "Britain and America respect the right
of all people to choose the form of government under which they will
live, and they wish to see sovereign rights and self-government
restored to those who have been forcibly deprived of them." Millions
of people have died thinking they were defending that principle.
Now men and women who dare to inscribe that principle on their
banners are shot down by the "defenders of democracy".

There are massacres every day now in Indo-China, India and
Java. The men who sit in judgment on the murderers of Lidice are
ordering Javanese villages to be burnt to the ground as reprisals.

What is the crime of these "extremists", of these "rebels", of
these "undesirable elements" and "rioters"? Pandit Nehru declared
a few days ago in Lahore: "Four hundred million Indians can
no longer tolerate British domination. We are now very impatient
to throw away the yoke of slavery. We are now terribly sick of the
British Government; we say 'go to hell'."

"Go to hell" echo the Indian masses. "You have robbed us of
our riches, you have forced our women and children down the
mines". "Go to hell" echo the Indo-Chinese people, "you are protecting French business people and officials who have starved us for
generations, who have poisoned us with opium and alcohol in order
to increase their profits." "Go to hell" cry the Indonesians, "we have
worked on tea and rubber plantations at starvation wages, we have

been sent to terror-ridden concentration camps in the jungle of New Guinea the moment we dared to protest."

In 1938 the profits the Dutch firms derived from their richest enterprises were over £25 million. The wages in Dutch concerns for a ten hour day ranged from two shillings and sixpence to seven and six a week. The average income of the inhabitants of the colony was a penny farthing a day. This is not propaganda put out by "extremists", they are figures published by the International Labour Office. No amount of bombing of Indonesian radio stations can destroy these terrible facts.

What answer does the Dutch Government give to these accusations of exploitation and oppression? There is Queen Wilhelmina's sickening, hypocritical speech from the throne at the opening of the Netherlands Provisional Parliament:

" I deeply regret the sufferings which inevitably overtakes the population of Java until order has been restored.

We are continuing to try to salvage the future of this ravaged land for the Dutch and for the Indonesians—the future of a commonwealth built on the voluntarily accepted solidarity of all parts of the empire."

The "voluntarily accepted solidarity" has already manifested itself in thousands of casualties among British and Indian troops and the Dutch and Indonesian civilian population.

The excuse for British intervention—that India, Indo-China and the Dutch Indies are not fit for democracy—is farcical. Is Portugal with its fake elections a democracy? Is Spain with its prisons swarming with political prisoners a democracy? Is Poland, ruled by the G.P.U.? Is Hungary, under the heel of Butcher Horthy? Yet all those countries are recognised by Britain as independent and we are proud to call Portugal our oldest ally!

The Chairman of the Labour Party, Professor Harold Laski, has condemned the policy of the Government in Indonesia and Indo-China. He said: "It makes the British claim to have been engaged in a war for democracy and freedom a hollow mockery all over South East Asia." If this represents the view of the Labour Party why is a Labour Government ordering British and Indian troops to shoot down and bomb Indonesians and Indo-Chinese? Why is it putting

the French and the Dutch back in the position where they can ruthlessly exploit millions of people who have clearly shown their hatred
of foreign rule?

The shedding of blood in South East Asia must be stopped.   No
faith can be put in the Labour Government.   They have shown themselves cold-blooded imperialists like any Tory Government.   America
is standing aloof supplying lend-lease weapons to crush the Indonesians, but letting Britain do the dirty work.   Russia, so articulate on
the question of the atomic bomb, has refrained from coming out on
the side of the colonial people.

The only effective help has come, and must continue to come,
from the workers.   The Australian workers who have refused to
handle supplies for the Dutch, the British seamen who refused to
carry Dutch troops, have shown the way.

When Britain tried to crush the Russian revolution, dockers
refused to load the *Jolly George* with munitions.   Bevin was with
the dockers then.   Our answer to him now must be in the spirit which
animated the dockers of the *Jolly George*:

Not a soldier—not a round of ammunition—not a machine gun—
not a plane for British intervention in Asia.

December, 1945.

31.   BRITISH ARMY OF OPPRESSION CRUSHES EASTERN FREEDOM

THE INK of the Peace terms, which were supposed to put an end to
totalitarianism, was not yet dry when American, British, French and
Dutch imperialisms hurried to take over the whip with which the
Japanese Government held the Indonesian and Indo-Chinese under
subjection.

Though the size of the territories where the revolts are taking
place cannot be compared with that of India, it would be a mistake to
underrate their importance.   The Indonesian archipelago is thickly
populated and has 7 million inhabitants, of which 50 million are in
the island of Java.   Of these only a quarter of a million are Europeans.

What is more important, the Dutch East Indies produces a great proportion of essential commodities. *Tribune* gives the following figures: 40 per cent. of the world's rubber, 17 per cent. of copra, large quantities of petroleum, tea, sugar and coffee, and practically the total world output of quinine come from there.

The exploitation of Indonesian riches and Indonesian cheap labour has always been extremely profitable to Holland which derived from it a yearly income of £40,000,000. This not only explains why the Dutch are anxious to maintain their hold on their colonies, but also the interest shown by Britain and America. At present 80 per cent. of the capital invested in the Dutch Indies comes from Holland. No doubt British and American capitalists would like to see their share of investments increased. By sending troops and armaments to crush the revolt they put the Dutch Government in their debt and pave the way to bigger investments. This is what one should understand from Attlee's declaration that we have obligations towards our great ally Holland. It is also obvious that it is in the interests of British Imperialism to crush any movement of independence in Asia. Were the Indonesians to throw the Dutch out, the event would have tremendous repercussions in other colonial countries. Throughout the Far East the happenings in Java are closely watched. From Singapore to Sydney, large scale dockyard strikes have taken place in sympathy with the movement, and a cable from India announces that: "Since Britain seems determined to use Indian troops and material for crushing Asiatic Freedom Movements, India feels the time has come to use its national strength in answer. Nation-wide preparations are already under way for rendering succour to its brother-peoples."

The campaign of lies and defamation which has accompanied the use of naked force in the Far East equals anything Goebbels might have engineered. The movement of national independence has been represented as having been hatched by the Japanese, in spite of the fact that the Indonesian Republic was not established until August 17, 1945, that is to say, after the Japanese surrender. The National Movement was born as long ago as 1912 and organised revolts in 1926 and 1927 which the Dutch repressed ruthlessly. The present nationalist leaders have all been imprisoned by the Dutch Government at various times.

The other lie is that British troops were used in order to protect Dutch civilian internees and prisoners of war against the violence of the extremists. The Japanese suddenly became the guardian angels of the Dutch, while blood-curdling stories of atrocities by Indonesians were published in the newspapers. The *News of the World* correspondent cabled from Batavia that:

"In towns and villages, in remote little homes, millions to-night in Java are lying awake in terror, praying for the speedy arrival of British troops. Order has broken down. The only law is that of the mob, the gun and the knife. Ordinary human decency has been cast aside . . . 50,000 Dutch women and children, interned under Japanese rule are at the mercy of crazed natives."

When one remembers that the total white population in Indonesia is half a million as against 70 million Indonesians one will realise that the "crazed natives" must be behaving pretty well since the casualties among the whites have been very small. The same correspondent who gives such a lurid picture of conditions in Java says later that he has made a 100 mile trip into the interior of the island, his only protection being apparently a Union Jack!

Another argument used against the Indonesians is that the Dutch government has offered self-government to the country in any case and that the Indonesians should therefore be good boys and they will get all they demand. Similar promises were made after the first world war and the Indonesians know what to expect from such promises. They fully realise that independence will not be given to them by the Dutch government or any other, and that they will have to wrest it by force if they want it.

After six years of war "for democracy" the British Labour Government is using British and (supreme irony) Indian troops to suppress movements which fight for the principles of the Atlantic Charter. The reasons given by the Government for doing so do not stand a minute's examination as we have already demonstrated.

To expose the hypocrisy still further there is General de Gaulle's declaration at a press conference in Washington on 24th August, 1945:

"The position of France regarding Indo-China," he said, "is very simple. France intends to recover her sovereignty over Indo-China.

Of course, she also intends to introduce a new régime, but for us, sovereignty is the major question. Indo-China must have an Indo-Chinese Government composed of Indo-Chinese as well as of Frenchmen residing in Indo-China, and presided over by the representative of France."

These are the intentions of France. The intentions of the British are shown by the presence of Seaforth Highlanders shooting down Indonesians. America has not sent troops, but has been sending war material as was admitted by Mr. Byrnes at his press conference in Washington on 24th October. He stated that "Britain and the Netherlands Government had been asked to strip United States emblems from all lend-lease equipment in Indonesia". And Mr. Byrnes added cynically, "This was a matter of general policy applying throughout the world wherever lend-lease material was used if there was a political connotation in its use."

While American bullets were shooting down Indonesians, President Truman announced the twelve fundamental points of U.S. foreign policy. Point 4 reads:

"We believe that all peoples who are prepared for self-government should be permitted to choose their own form of government by their own freely expressed choice without interference from any foreign source. This is true in Europe, in Asia, and in Africa, as well as in the Western Hemisphere."

This blatant piece of hypocrisy was skipped by the B.B.C. in their broadcast of the 12 points; it was too much even for the B.B.C.!

The Labour Government has shown that it will pursue an imperialist policy worthy of any Tory government. The Trade Union Congress in Paris has shown that the Trade Unions of the home countries share the imperialist aims of their governments and look with hostility on the Trade Unions of colonial countries when these show aspirations towards independence. The Communist Party adopts an anti-imperialist policy merely when it suits Russia. It is anti-imperialist as far as the Far East is concerned and Mr. Togliatti, the Communist Minister of Justice in Italy, declared that colonies have always been a liability to Italy and that they should be relinquished, but a few days afterwards Russia announced that she wanted to co-operate in the administration of Italian colonies!

The British Government attacks French imperialism in Syria but defends it in Indo-China. Moscow attacks Dutch imperialism but wants its share of Italian colonies. "Freedom" acquires a different meaning when it is a question of buying up petrol interests or of defending rubber plantations.

The war in the Far East does not only disprove all the lofty idealism for which the present war is supposed to have been fought. It is the beginning of a new and fiercer war which will bring mass destruction among the colonial people as well as ourselves. Will millions of people again be sacrificed for rubber, tin, sugar, petrol, and tea interests?

November, 1945.

32. THE GREAT FARCE OF SAN FRANCISCO

WHAT IS really surprising about the San Francisco conference is not that it is a demonstration of power politics. We all expected that, behind the humanitarian speeches and the resolutions of good will; behind the pretence of planning a world free from war and oppression, the cynical sharing out of power, the deadly chess game of secret diplomacy would be preparing the scene for the next open contest of physical power for the domination of the world. What we did not expect was that the chess board would be brought so much into the open, and the game of power played with such an open disregard for the old diplomatic pretences.

Such a conference as this has a dual aspect. In one purpose, that of joining together to keep the power of their class intact, the participants will act in unison. They will all agree to any measures that are likely to make more difficult, or to crush out, any real revolutionary movement among the peoples of the world. The one prospect they regard with horror is that their power will be torn from their hands, and an era of real freedom, goodwill, and peace will arise from the co-operation of peoples freed from the rule of politicians and generals. Therefore we can take it that, however much disunity there may appear to be amongst the participants in the conference, they will unite on this one issue, and that the certain result of the conference is some kind of new Holy Alliance directed against revolutionary movements wherever they may arise in the world.

But the fact that they are united in this one desire does not mean that they will not quarrel between themselves as to the division of the power that is to be wielded over the workers of the world. Indeed, one thing that has been obvious from the beginning of the conference has been the bitterness of the division of interests between the great powers who dominate the conference, and the way in which the need for united action against possible revolutionary movements is actually being used as an instrument for bargaining between the various powers.

From its beginning, the conference has been an illustration of the old diplomatic proverb that 'Might is Right'. This was first shown in the sharp division of function and weight between the four 'big powers' and the remaining delegations, whose rôle is rendered somewhat superfluous by the power of veto granted to the great powers. This distinction was, moreover, shown in a dramatic way by the fact that the representatives of the four great powers were divided from the small countries by sitting against an elaborate background on the stage of the San Francisco Opera House. There is to be no doubt as to who are the stars in this uncomfortably realistic Green Table ballet.

That the participants in the conference were not idealistic in their motives was obvious from the beginning. In an early report (27th April), the *News Chronicle* correspondent remarked:

"It would be less than honest not to recognise that the conference is being attended by some delegations and a good many pressure groups who have axes to grind and would like to use this occasion to grind them."

The squabbles began almost immediately, and Molotov showed without any hesitation that the Russian Government intended to leave no doubt of its power and its intentions. In the beginning there was a difference over the chairmanship, the American delegation wishing to keep this influential position. This was settled by a compromise largely in favour of the Americans, for while the chairmanships of the plenary sessions was to be taken in turns, the chairmanships of the Steering and Executive Committees were retained by Stettinius. Molotov then demanded separate representation for the Ukraine and White Russia, thereby showing that the object of the granting of nominal national status to the constituent republics of the U.S.S.R. some time ago was, as we said at the time, to gain bargaining power in conferences for the Russian government. This somewhat cynical demand was granted. The American group, more obviously than ever dominated by the U.S.A. since the Chapultepec conference, brought forward the Argentine as a makeweight. Molotov objected to the Argentine because it was not democratic (!) but seemed inclined to waive the question of its democracy or otherwise if he were allowed to bring in a delegate of the Lublin Polish Committee. The vote on the admission of the Argentine showed the alignment of the conflicting power groups. Apart from the two obvious puppet delegations, the Russians had the support of three Eastern European nations: Czechoslovakia, Yugoslavia and Greece. The U.S.A. had the support of the Latin American countries as well as most of the British dominions. France and Belgium, unsure of their ground, and fearful of Russia as well as of the Anglo-American temporary alliance, abstained from voting.

The first few days of what is supposed to be a conference of historic importance for the future benefit of humanity have thus been consumed almost entirely with manœuvres to gain influence. The Russian government in these initial stages showed their intentions of gaining as much as possible by the most cynical use of any means at their disposal. This does not mean that the British and American governments are any less anxious to gain influence and use the conference for the purposes of the interests they represent. But they have moved carefully, according to their traditional methods of an occult diplomacy in which the brutal reality of power is revealed only in absolute necessity, while the Russians have been quite open in their display of the kind of imperialist power tactics, the mixture of bullying and bluff, which until recently were associated with the vanished Nazi leaders. Bolshevik Russia is revealed more openly than ever as an expanding imperialist power whose claim to act in the interests of the workers is patently cynical and conceived in bad faith.

The differences between the conflicting powers have continued to deepen. Molotov has already, like a slighted prima donna, announced his intention of leaving the conference in the near future, and on the 5th May a further crisis developed when the British and the Americans broke off their talks with the Russians over the Polish question because of the imprisonment of the sixteen Polish representatives who had gone to discuss political questions with the Russian authorities in March. The Russian government, forced into the open, has published a statement of the kind to which we are used in these days of naïve political lying.

"General Okulicki's group," says the Tass agency, "and especially he himself, are accused of preparing diversionary acts in the rear of the Red Army, as a result of which more than 100 officers and men of the Red Army lost their lives.

This group of 16 persons did not disappear, but were arrested by the military authorities of the Soviet Command and are now in Moscow pending the investigation of the case.

The group is also accused of the installation and maintenance in the rear of Soviet troops of illegal radio transmitters, which constitutes an act punishable by law. All these persons, or some of them, as the investigations may warrant, will be committed for trial."

It becomes more clear than ever before that the real point of the San Francisco conference is not the prevention of war or the bringing of prosperity back to the world, but merely the division of power for the time being between the major groups. The seeds of the next war are no doubt being sown, but be it remembered that the various ruling classes will not willingly let their differences become so deep that they will relax their attack on their common enemy, the working people of every country. The San Francisco conference will undoubtedly be a disappointment for those who expect it to bring justice, freedom or material well-being. But, at least, for the time being, it will probably fulfil its real purpose of establishing the share-out of power between England, America, and Russia. And it will at least have performed the service of demonstrating beyond a doubt the openly imperialist intentions of the present Russian ruling class.

May, 1945.

33. FAMINE AND POLITICAL CRISIS: BACKGROUND TO BIG THREE MEETING

TRUMAN, CHURCHILL and Stalin are meeting this week in Berlin. This event is the logical consummation of the war. It is also, and above all, the first phase of a new political era. To-day Europe wants to start life again. And these gentlemen of Washington and London and Moscow wish to reach agreement on the rule they intend to impose on this new Europe. They wish to draw frontiers, to authorise or forbid the rebirth of parties or political movements. But, before anything else, they wish to talk business. For Europe to-day is not only a mass of ruins. It is a field for exploitation. It contains raw materials and markets. It also contains strategic positions.

San Francisco and its organisation to abolish war do not seem to inspire any confidence even among those who are charged to ensure its functioning. Stalin in particular seeks to establish himself firmly in Central, Eastern, and Southern Europe, in order, if necessary, to hold in check his British and American "friends". Churchill views the Russian manœuvres with a certain restlessness. Truman represents American business, which is anxious to secure its part of the booty. And here they are at Berlin, or rather at Potsdam, the cradle of Prussian militarism. They meet in particularly favourable circumstances. The Entente is victorious. Unfortunately, it is not cordial.

It was understood that Berlin would be a kind of international city, and that it would be occupied jointly by the Great Powers. On that point agreement was reached at Yalta, and the Russians gave their word.

It is now some days since the flag of His Majesty was hoisted in Berlin. But just below the historic photographs showing the triumphant march of British troops through the streets of Berlin, the newspapers published an order of the day from General Wales, one of the commanders of the English forces in which the General said to his soldiers:

"For some reason which I myself do not know, there was a misunderstanding between our own government and that of our Russian Allies, and no accommodation for troops under my command was provided."

In other words, the Russian allies have received the British allies as unwelcome guests.

It is unpleasant enough to have to sleep in the streets, especially when one is the conqueror. But that is not all. In this order of the day, which was read at the time of the parade, General Wales also said:

"Our Russian Allies have developed an extremely high standard of security, which they have clearly decided to maintain in spite of the fact that the hostilities have ceased."

Thus the army of His Britannic Majesty will be treated not only as a band of uninvited beggars, but also as suspects on whom it is necessary to keep an eye. The Russian Committee of reception is composed more than anything else of agents of the G.P.U. The atmosphere is thus excellent for an historic conference!

That is the background. And what is the business to be transacted? Truman, Churchill and Stalin have first to decide the problems of Germany. Among these are certain questions on which agreement is very far from having been reached.

Because of geographical circumstances, it happens that the Russians occupy the principal agricultural districts of Germany. It is to be anticipated that want or famine will exist most of all in the French, English, and American zones.

Stalin has been very ready to seize the political advantages conferred by this situation. It is obvious that the Russians intend to speculate on the fact that under their rule people eat, while under the western Allies they suffer from hunger. *War Commentary* has already given certain indications of Russian policy in this respect: the building up of stocks for the German people, the increase in rations to the people of Berlin by the Soviet commander, the efforts of Mikoyan, the second-in-command of the Soviet régime, who goes out of his way to inspect the material conditions of Germany. Now there is more to say.

Besides the agents of the G.P.U. there was among the reception committee for the Anglo-American troops in Berlin, a certain Dr. Arthur Werner who fulfils the functions of mayor under the Russians. In a pretence of welcome, he said: "We have awaited the arrival of the British and Americans with great anticipation because we expect them to send us food." This statement amounts to a simple provo-cation, in view of the fact that the English and the Americans have openly stated that they will not help Germany. Moreover, Truman has just proposed that the Germans should be forced to produce coal for the 'liberated' countries of Europe.

Then the spokesman of the Russian administration added a little threat: "America is such a rich country and eventually America certainly will be interested in re-establishing trade with Germany."

There Dr. Werner touched a sentimental chord. Obviously the U.S.A. wishes to re-establish its commercial relations with Germany. Without that, would it have been worth the trouble of making war? But behind the mayor of Berlin, the Russians intended to speak to their dear allies. Either you help the Germans and put yourselves in bad odour with other European countries (incidentally, the Com-munist parties in these countries would be the first to denounce such aid), or you do not aid the Germans, and then we shall have an easy game because the Germans will consider you as oppressors, and it will then be difficult for you to do business with them.

The latest news from Berlin indicates that the Russian authorities have brought to a head the question of feeding the Germans. The British and American armies of occupation have found that the Russians are still maintaining virtual control of all Berlin until the Western Allies consent to send food into Germany. The Russian troops may have moved out of the districts in question, but the whole German machine of administration is still working to the orders of the Russian authorities, and it has been made clear that this will continue until agreement has been reached on the food question.

Thus everything is perfect for the conference of the Three Great Powers. All the more so as Stalin is already solving, in his own manner, the German political problem. The German Communist Party has been reconstituted and is quick to declare itself against socialism. The Social Democrats and the Catholics have also been authorised to resume their activities in the Russian zone. The German middle class begin to understand that the red flag with the hammer and sickle no longer means revolution.

But one knows nothing for certain of what happens in the Russian zone. In other zones, there is complete chaos. Poverty grows from day to day. Hate against the occupying Powers unites all sections of public opinion. The British authorities show by their brutality that they are nothing but conquerors. The French demand that the German population shall salute each allied soldier by raising their hats when they pass. The displaced persons, Poles, Jugoslavs and Italians continue to live in camps under conditions which are far from good.

The Potsdam Conference is meeting at a time when throughout Europe political crises are developing. Belgium, France, and Greece, Spain, Tangier and Czechoslovakia, Poland, and Turkey are all on the order of the day.

Russia has already occupied important strategical positions. Sub-Carpathian Ruthenia has been incorporated in the Ukraine. Poland is docile. Jugoslavia is an "ally". Now Stalin is putting pressure on Turkey to decide in a "satisfactory" manner the question of the entrance to the Black Sea.

And the City is uneasy, and its anxiety is not lessened by the Russian demand to take part in the administration of Tangier.

The conference at Potsdam is meeting under very favourable circumstances indeed.

July, 1945.

34.   CRISIS OVER EUROPE

IF WE needed any convincing that the immediate future of Europe is to be the battle-ground for conflicting power politics, we should have gained it from the conference of Foreign Ministers in London. The physical struggle which led to the destruction of the Nazis is to be followed by a political and diplomatic struggle of no less bitterness, backed by the open threat of force and the unprincipled use of any economic or political weapon that lies to the hand of the conflicting political groups. The ending of the war has dispelled, like a fog in a gale, any pretence of unity that had previously existed among the Allies.

The most sensational event of the conference was the Russian demand for a share of the Italian colonies, in opposition to the

American suggestion of some form of international trusteeship. Here the contrasting aims of these two most formidable of the "great" powers became evident. The Americans, with a top-heavy capitalist structure, are interested in free markets, and prefer international controls or even nominal independence of backward countries to an imperialist domination that will oppose their own economic interests. The Russians, on the other hand, are interested in extending their power bases into the Mediterranean and the Red Sea coast. The *Daily Worker*, attempting to justify Molotov's actions, remarked with a truly virginal air of offended innocence:

"Why was the Soviet proposal to take over the trusteeship of certain Italian colonies greeted with such an astonished outcry? It is, indeed, surprising that Soviet willingness to undertake additional international obligations, to help colonial peoples forward to independence and to play a part in guaranteeing security in the Mediterranean was not welcomed with open arms by all upholders of international co-operation."

Indeed, before such a rebuke we blush with shame ever to have thought evil of such gentle and noble creatures as Comrades Stalin and Molotov. Of course, they have everybody's interest at heart but their own! Nevertheless, we cannot help remembering what Lenin said about colonies, and the fact that the Atlantic Charter, which was endorsed by the Russians, declared that the Allied Powers sought "no aggrandisement, territorial or other". Such a complete reversal of declared Soviet policy and ancient Marxist principles can only be explained by a desire on the part of the Russian ruling class to gain and consolidate the power over Europe which they have already established in the countries on Russia's Eastern border.

Meanwhile, the fate of any colonials who decided that they did not want kind Soviet guardianship can be judged from the attitude of the authorities of Russia and the Balkan countries towards displaced persons and other refugees whom they regard as being technically their subjects. At the meeting of the U.N.R.R.A. Council last month in London, the delegates of Russia, Poland, Jugoslavia, and Czechoslovakia demanded that U.N.R.R.A. should cease providing relief for displaced persons who refused to return to their countries. They asked that political refugees should be offered the alternative of starving or of returning to certain persecution in Communist-dominated countries. Similar requests have been made by the Jugo-slav government to the British authorities in Italy regarding the 20,000 political refugees who are sheltering there. So far, the other countries have refused to accede to such a blatant request that political oppositionists should be handed over for extermination. As the American *New Leader* remarked:

"Russia was demanding here that the principle of compulsion which exists in Soviet territory be acknowledged by the other nations of the world. They refused. If they hadn't, the ancient right of political asylum which has sheltered, although inadequately, the victims of Nazism would have been abolished."

The "democratic" countries of the West have not yet arrived at such a state of authoritarianism that they are willing openly to declare themselves the enemies of freedom of opinion.

But although the Allied governments have not reached agreement on the Russian demand for extradition of political opponents, they have accepted the Russian principle of forced labour, as applied to the German people in particular. Probably no action of the Nazis was exposed to such violent criticism as the policy of carrying millions of people away from their homes and their countries and subjecting them to forced labour. Yet now, the "enemies of Nazism" are using the same policy, for in the proclamation of the Allied Commanders-in-Chief in Germany there is a clause—No. 19—which states categorically that:

"the German authorities . . . will provide such transport, plant, equipment, and materials of all kinds, labour, personnel, and specialist and other services for use *in Germany or elsewhere* as the Allied representatives may direct."

The 'democratic powers' have given in to Russia on yet another point—the recognition of the puppet Hungarian Government. A few weeks back, Bevin included Hungary in his list of countries to be denounced because their constitutions were undemocratic. Yet last week-end the American government suddenly recognised the Hungarian government, and it is expected that its lead will be followed

by the British. Has the Hungarian government, which is the same
as it was a few weeks ago, suddenly changed its opinions and actions?
Or is it possible that the Western allies see in Hungary a potential
bastion of influence which they may use to undermine Russian power
in Eastern Europe?

Meanwhile, as the background to this dance of the rulers, the
people of Europe are starving, and millions are faced with certain
death from famine and cold, while in other parts of the world there
are ample supplies of food to satisfy their needs and sufficient transport to bring it to their doors. At this moment 'The Beast of Belsen'
is facing a court where he is being asked why he let the thousands
of prisoners under his charge starve to death while there was food
nearby that would have saved their lives. Beside him in the dock
should stand all the rulers of the countries of the world, who with
an abundance of food at their command, are allowing the people of
Europe to starve while they spar among themselves for political power
and exterminate whatever opposition arises to resist them.

October, 1945.

35. U.N.O.—A SCREEN FOR POLITICAL INTRIGUE

TWENTY-SIX YEARS ago the League of Nations came into existence,
and, however much cynical calculation on the part of politicians may
have gone towards its formation, there is no doubt that a great deal
of idealism was to be found amongst its active protagonists, and that
very great numbers of the people in many countries looked to its
future activities with faith and optimism. To-day the United
Nations opens its sessions, and nothing is more evident than the
complete and open cynicism of the politicians and executives who
direct its activities, which is balanced by an equally evident distrust
and pessimism on the part of the peoples of the world.

In spite of Attlee's statement that U.N.O. "must become the over-
riding factor in foreign policy", it is already evident, as the *Manchester Guardian* has pointed out, that "there will always be a tendency
for the Great Powers to decide the more important—or more delicate

—matters outside the organisation". The very nature of the U.N.O. organisation, with the importance attached to the voices of the Great Powers, and the slight influence granted to minor countries, is bound to encourage the more powerful countries to disregard the minor ones and treat their opinions with contempt.

It is significant that the British Government has chosen to bring before the new World Court a ridiculous minor dispute with Guatemala. The disagreement concerns the delimitation of the frontier between Guatemala and British Honduras, and has been unsettled since 1859. One would have thought that a matter which had waited for over eighty years could stand aside for weightier matters. But no, this hoary dispute whose originators have long been in their graves has to be dragged out of its cupboard while the urgent problems of Europe and the Far East are tacitly ignored.

The question of Germany, with her starving millions of home- less refugees, for instance, has not been brought forward yet, except by the Danish delegate, whose references to this problem were met with silence among the countries directly concerned with the adminis- tration of Germany. According to Vernon Bartlett: "Uncertainty about this country's future is still the major obstacle to agreement between the permanent members of the Security Council", and it is evident that the politicians of the great powers consider international peace less important than trying to make the best deal they can for themselves out of this and other major problems.

These instances show clearly the futility of the activities of U.N.O. as an organisation for the maintenance of world peace or safeguarding the welfare of the peoples of the world. Its delegates, and most of all the delegates of the Great Powers who virtually con- trol it, are concerned to preserve it as a façade to hide their own real political activities. In questions which affect their own interests directly, the United Nations as a whole will be allowed very little say. This was made blatantly clear by the statements of Gromyko, the Russian representative, who stated that the U.N.O. would succeed if the Big Three continued to act in a spirit of unanimity and con- cord. The *Manchester Guardian* report of his speech goes on:

"Small nations must be kept in their place; the General Assem- bly must not try to usurp the powers and privileges of the Security

Council. The revival of the methods applied in the League of Nations would cause nothing but harm."

In other words, the Russian government is interested in the United Nations only as a stage for the wrangles of the imperialist powers to take place under cover of a specious nationalism. The real contempt with which the Kremlin regards the U.N.O. is shown by the fact that Molotov has not chosen to attend the meetings, that at the time of writing Vyshinsky has not yet arrived, and that such a minor figure as Gromyko should act as leading representative. Stalin means to indicate from the outset that he is not taking any orders from U.N.O.

There is no doubt that Russia's attitude is largely motivated by the fact that the Persian dispute is coming up for consideration by the Security Council. But in fact, the Security Council has little real power in this matter, for, although Russia may be required not to vote on the Council's decision, as a party to the dispute, the Kremlin government can still impose its veto on any decision taken by the Security Council to implement its views.

In any case, it seems unlikely that the U.N.O. will touch on the fundamental points of the Persian dispute.* Political questions will be discussed, the withdrawal of Russian troops, the revision of electoral laws, the granting of language rights to minorities, etc. But there is no indication that the discussion of the U.N.O. will touch upon the fundamental economic issues.

The real cause of the Persian dispute is the struggle between the great powers for oil resources. The Middle East—Persia, Iraq. and Arabia—contains in the neighbourhood of 30 per cent. of the world's oil resources, and the real cause of the Persian dispute was the desire of Russia to break in on this great reservoir of oil before the rival interests of British and American companies, backed by their respective governments, had gained complete control.

Any decision of the Security Council is likely to have little effect on the Persian issue, because the major activity of the Russian government was not concerned with direct intervention. The Russian troops merely played an incidental rôle to ensure the success of the

*This must not be confused with the present dispute between the Persian Government and the Anglo-Iranian Oil Company.—EDITOR.

major plan of indirect intervention by internal disruption. The Russians began their real attack on Persia by causing the foundation of the Tudeh, a pseudo-progressive party whose real object was to further Russian interests. When this failed to gain the Russian objective of oil concessions by constitutional action, the Russians formed a new party, the Democrats, which resorted to armed revolt in order to force a favourable attitude to Russia on the part of the Persian government. It would be possible for the Russians to make a hypocritical gesture by withdrawing all Red Army troops, and still to retain the main influence on Persia through the semi-quisling movements which have formed and have so far maintained Russian interests very effectively. In these circumstances the United Nations, even if they wished, could do nothing to stop the spread of Russian influence, and we should be back at the point where the British and Americans, on their own account, would be trying to beat the Russians at the same game.

While it is evident that the United Nations will be completely useless as a means of maintaining world peace, or of attaining any benefits for the workers of the world, there is at least one class of people who will benefit by it. These are the bureaucrats and politicians. Already it has been made public that the Secretary-General will receive £9,000 a year, tax free, for his services, and an enormous staff of similarly over-paid officials is being formed, so that, we are informed, the B.B.C. is emptying itself into the United Nations because of the very high salaries given to translators and secretaries.

The starvation and misery of the millions in Europe and the Far East can only be made the more bitter by the spectacle of this orgy of futile speech-making and cynical self-advancement.

January, 1946.

36. U.N.O. CANNOT PREVENT WAR

IN AMERICA the delegates to the so-called United Nations are meeting in an atmosphere of luxurious living and bureaucratic extravagance. A vast and growing army of officials, already 3,000 in number and increasing daily, draw large salaries and live in plenty, ministered to by many servants and lackeys, and guarded by a private police force. Trygve Lie, secretary-general of the organisation, we are told, has two large mansions which are paid for by the organisation—one to live in, the other to eat his lunch in. He has a heated and air-conditioned limousine, equipped with radio, and his standard of living generally is maintained on this luxury level.

These facts give the tone of the gathering at which the fate of many millions of workers, for decades to come, will be decided. It is a gathering which meets in an atmosphere of unreality, intentionally divorced from the real life of the people in all countries. Against this scene of luxurious living, of political manœuvring, of insincerity carried to an extreme, the lives of the common people of the world stand out in misery and horror.

In this issue of *Freedom* alone we publish accounts of life in four countries—Spain, Italy, Germany and South Africa—where the workers are living in starvation and oppression. The list could be extended almost indefinitely, to include the people of China and Japan, the Russian workers, the negroes of Harlem only a short distance away from the meeting place of the United Nations itself.

Wherever we look in the world, we see the ruling classes of the Allied countries pursuing a foreign policy that seems to be inspired either by wanton folly or by the callous intention of making the lives of the people in the more unfortunate countries even worse than they are to-day.

Let us take Spain as an example. To-day there are "democratic' governments in power in Britain, France and America. The leaders of these governments have paid lip-service to the cause of Spanish freedom, have made grandiloquent speeches against Franco and his régime, but so far they have not done a thing towards the overthrow of the military tyranny in Spain, or to help the Spanish people in their struggle against Franco. The Trades Union Congress, itself now something very near a representative organ of the ruling class, gave a typical example of reformist handling of the Spanish situation. A resolution was passed demanding the breaking of diplomatic and economic relations with Spain. But in all the debate that led up to this resolution and in the resolution itself there was not a single suggestion of assistance or practical support for the Spanish people themselves. And without support for their struggle the Spanish people will be the first to suffer from an economic blockade. In any case, it remains to be seen whether this resolution means anything, and whether the Trade Union leaders will in fact apply pressure to the government to take any kind of action that might embarrass Franco.

The treatment of Italy by the Allied powers is another example of the way in which governments carry on their political game without regard for the interests of the people concerned. To quote one example of this treatment: in the revision of the Franco-Italian frontier, two Italian power stations are now in French territory. These power stations serve only Italian towns and villages, and are of no practical use at all to the French, but for the future the Italians will have to pay tribute to the French government for their use. This is a great loss to a people whose country contains little coal and relies very largely on hydro-electric power.

Another example is that of the Italian navy. This navy was never surrendered—it was voluntarily placed at the disposal of the Allied powers, and did a good deal of fighting on their behalf against the German forces. Yet the ships are now to be taken away and shared out among the various Allies, and, what concerns us primarily, the sailors will be thrown into unemployment without compensation, to swell the ranks of the millions of half-starved workless people in Italy to-day.

But the mere lack of consideration for the material needs of the peoples of the world is not the only threatening feature of the policy of the various allied governments. To this must be added the continual war of nerves which is being carried on by these governments, in order to keep the people tuned to the idea of war. The action of the Russian government last week, of deporting German technicians to Russia on the eve of the United Nations Conference seems almost calculated to arouse antagonism and to present issues around which the talk of war could grow and add to the unsureness of the people. This is only one example of the long series of provocative gestures, not confined to one side or one nation, which have precipitated the people of the world into a condition of despair regarding the possibility of avoiding war.

Clearly, the Allied governments do not regard peace as important. More important to them is to keep the people continually on edge, to have renewed excuses for maintaining their insecure economic systems on a war footing, for continuing to impose conscription, and for maintaining their class systems of privilege which will allow luxury of the kind prevalent at the U.N.O. conference to exist in all the capitals of the world, side by side with the starvation and fear of further wars which afflict the workers everywhere.

We are assured by politician after politician that there will be no war. First Stalin and then Truman give us these benign assurances. But neither we nor the majority of the workers are blind to the signs of the times. People fear the possibility of war, and they are right to do so while the governments of the world are allowed to carry on their policies of imperialist rivalry. The politicians tell us there will be no more war, but at the same time they spread the rumours of war, they make the gestures which lead up to war. It can be taken almost as a natural law in politics, that a politician does not think of denying the likelihood of war unless that likelihood is very much on his mind. The policies of America, Russia, France, and England alike lead only to one end—the maintenance of an imperialist war economy, and the efforts of the various rivals in this field can lead only to an eventual war far more destructive than the last, unless the workers themselves realise in time what is in store for them and refuse all over the world to obey the insane dictates of their masters, of whatever race or political creed.

November, 1946.

37. FUTILITY IN FRANCE

DURING THE past two weeks the Foreign Ministers in London have devoted a few hours a day to discussing the share of their respective countries in the spoils of the Second World War. Little interest has been taken in this meeting, partly because it was considered as being doomed to failure, partly because the limelight was stolen by the activities of the Communists in France and to a lesser extent in Italy.

The impression created was that the fate of Europe was not being decided round the conference table but in the factories and streets of France. It was Moscow's way of showing that, if it was in the minority at the conference, it was strong enough to make trouble in countries supposedly in the sphere of influence of the other great powers.

The sensationalist Press described the agitation as a revolutionary struggle (a much abused expression these days) and as an attempt by the Communists to seize power. After several weeks of struggle against the government, the Communists have not seized power and, at the moment of writing, they seem to have lost considerable ground.

There is no evidence, however, that the Communist Party intended to carry out a full-scale insurrection. It is more likely that the agitation was considered suitable as a background for the negotiations taking place in London.

True, the Communists staged a stay-in strike in the French Assembly, but they behaved more like naughty schoolchildren determined to give their master a bad time, than dangerous revolutionaries. It is reckoned that, during one session, the Marseillaise was sung eight times, the Internationale twelve times and an old song calling to soldiers not to fire on strikers twenty-two times. The President of the Assembly used air-raid sirens to quell the uproar. While this Rag went on, strikers and demonstrators were being bludgeoned by the police, fired upon by the troops and jailed.

Outside Parliament the agitation was organised with that disregard for human sufferings and human lives which characterises the Party.

Acts of sabotage (some may have been the work of agents provocateurs as the C.P. asserts), and the use of arms and explosives, might have had their justification if they had been the prelude to revolution. As it was, they appear as senseless manifestations which merely served to strengthen the hand of reaction.

Anarchists, at least most of them, are not opposed to violence when it is made necessary by the revolutionary struggle. But when violence is used by a political party to refurbish its tarnished prestige, they condemn it as bringing unnecessary suffering to the people.

French and Italian workers have sufficient reasons to revolt without having to fight Stalin's battles. If they struck to defend their own interests, their sacrifices would not be in vain. They would then not march on orders received from Moscow and only go as far as their leaders allow them to go.

Anarchists believe that strikes must prepare the workers for the ultimate expropriation of the capitalist class. That is why they advocate the occupation of the factories, the direct exchange of goods between the countryside and the towns, the running of all means of communication for the benefit of the community. This would be a truly revolutionary agitation which would give workers confidence in their ability to run production, distribution and transport, through their own independent organisations. It would receive the support of the whole population (except for the small privileged minority), who now resent strikes which depress the already low level of production, which disorganise the distribution of food and make transport difficult and even dangerous.

In opposition to the "Molotov strikes", the French Anarchist movement advocates strikes for workers' control of industry. These are the strikes which will deal the heaviest blow to capitalism and political parties by putting power into the hands of the working-class.

December, 1947.

38. THE RUSSIAN ELECTIONS

FOR THE first time in eight years the Russian people have gone to the
polls to elect a new Supreme Soviet of the Union of Socialist Soviet
Republics. The Supreme Soviet consists of two Parliaments: The
Soviet of the Union and the Soviet of Nationalities and is elected
every four years.

The Soviet of the Union has 656 seats and is elected on the
basis of one deputy for every 300,000 of the population. The Soviet
of Nationalities has 631 seats on the basis of twenty-five deputies from
each constituent republic, irrespective of its size, eleven deputies from
each autonomous province and one deputy from each national region.
Voting is by universal suffrage for all who have reached the age of
eighteen, "irrespective of sex, nationality, race, faith, social origin,
property status or past activities". Candidates must be over twenty-
three years of age.

The Supreme Soviet of the U.S.S.R. elects a Presidium of the
Supreme Soviet of the U.S.S.R., composed of 37 members, and en-
dowed with great power. Theoretically the legislative power belongs
to the Supreme Soviet but the Presidium has the right to issue decrees
which have the power of law. The members of the Presidium cannot
be removed by the Supreme Soviet but they have the right to dissolve
the Supreme Soviet in case of an insoluble difference arising between
the Soviet of the Union and the Soviet of Nationalities.

The Supreme Soviet of the U.S.S.R. also appoints the highest
executive and administrative organ of State Power: the Council of
People's Commissars of the U.S.S.R. who deal with the international
organisation of the country.

The term Supreme Soviet is highly misleading. It has nothing
in common with the Soviets which were formed during the Russian
revolution and were councils of workers' delegates (or peasants and
soldiers) elected by a relatively small number of people and directly
responsible to them. The deputies in the Soviet of the Union each
represent something like three hundred thousand men and women
and remain in office for four years. Not a very direct kind of
representation!

What is the difference between the Russian parliamentary system
and that of democratic countries? The main difference is that under

the Soviet régime there are no opposition parties. The right to nominate candidates is reserved to official bodies that is to say, Communist
Party organisations, trade unions, co-operatives, organisations of youth,
cultural societies. The candidates who are not Communist Party
members are described as non-party but they are in fact supporters
of the Party. Stalin stressed the point, in his election broadcast on
9th February, that non-party people were now united with the
Communists in one common team of Soviet citizens which forged the
victory over their country's enemies.

"The only difference between them," said Stalin, "is that some
belong to the party while others do not. *But this is a formal difference*" (italics ours).

Under the Soviet system there is no chance to choose between
candidates representing two or more policies as there is only one
Party in the State, the Communist Party.

The choice of the candidates is not left to the electors at the
time of the election. Several candidates are nominated for each
constituency and except in constituencies which have such illustrious
candidates as Stalin, Molotov, Kalinin, Voroshilov, Zhukov, etc., a
certain amount of discussion takes place before the single candidate
is decided upon. Once he is chosen voting becomes a pure formality,
the only way to express opposition to the candidate is to abstain from
voting but as in the plebiscites organised in fascist countries—great
care is taken to get a maximum of voters to the polls (Age is no
excuse; in Georgia an old man of 118 went to the polls!).

In a police state such as Russia it is probable that more than
mere persuasion is used to ensure that the great majority of people
fill in their ballot papers though, of course, propaganda is used on
a big scale. It is aimed at giving the electors the illusion that they
have power to pass judgment on the Communist Party. At the
beginning of his speech Stalin declared: "The Communist Party
of our country would be of little worth were it not ready to accept
the electors' verdict." Having no rival parties to oppose it, being
supported by a Party-controlled Press and radio, having at its command the army, the police and millions of bureaucrats it would be
very difficult indeed to understand why the Communist Party should
be afraid of the electors' verdict.

No wonder Stalin's speech was "confident" (*Daily Worker*). He was spared the exhausting tours that politicians such as Churchill or Roosevelt had to undertake in order to secure re-election. Not for him the speeches on top of cars or standing in the rain; not for him the last minute Press campaign skilfully calculated to destroy weeks of propaganda work. Stalin's re-election was preceeded by a unanimous concert of praise. *Pravda*, for example, paid this inspired tribute:

"It is indeed happiness, real happiness, to meet Comrade Stalin. If one translated the endless acclamations into the language of simple words they would read: 'We are proud that the greatest man of our day, the brilliant creator of victory, the saviour of civilisation, the leader of the peoples, belongs to us, to our country, to our people. We know and are deeply convinced that the greatest man of our time could not appear in any other country but ours'."

And from Radio Khaborovsk (6/1/46):

"Yesterday's pre-election meeting in the Stalin precinct of Moscow left one with an unforgettable and inspiring impression. It reflected with great power and sincerity the boundless love the people bear for their great leader, wise teacher and father, Comrade Stalin!
'Dear Comrades', declares the woman worker A. A. Slobnow, 'it is the great fortune of our people that during the difficult years of the war it was Comrade Stalin, deputy of the entire people, who stood at the head of the state . . . Glory! Glory to our own J. V. Stalin.' These words are an expression of the innermost thoughts, feelings and hopes of the Soviet people."

When the votes were counted in Stalin's constituency in Moscow, it was found that 100 per cent. of the voters had cast their votes for Stalin.

Probably nobody dared to give Stalin the advice Kingsley Martin gave to Tito a few days before Yugoslavia's elections: "I hope you will get 75 per cent.," said K. Martin, "If you get 90 per cent., it might be a good idea to destroy 25 per cent. of your vote."

Stalin is different, of course, but 100 per cent. somehow does not sound very convincing.

February, 1946.

39. CHANGING SCENE IN RUSSIA

THOSE WHO imagine the totalitarian State as a wholly rigid structure
are quite mistaken. Perhaps in some future, dreamed of by dictators
and party leaders, when all men will have been conditioned from
birth, a naturally rigid society may ensue—although to me this seems
contrary to all our knowledge of the history and growth of human
organisations. However that may be, at present the dictator has no
rigid society on which to base his rule. He has to deal with mutable
and, from his point of view, very unreliable human beings. It is the
unpredictability of political life that forces a dictatorship, whatever
its apparent rigidity, to be involved in a constant inner flux, a continual changing of policy and reshuffling of personnel in order to
maintain the balance of forces that will keep the top crust still in
place.

The history of the Nazi dictatorship was such a story, and that
of the Russian Bolshevik government is an even more obvious case.
Not merely have almost all the old leaders of the Revolution—except
those who were fortunate enough to die naturally beforehand—been
liquidated, but whole succeeding generations of leaders have been
displaced in one way or another, and also the lower ranks of the
Communist Party have been subjected to such continual and violent
purges that even before the war, at the 18th Party Congress in 1939,
it was revealed that only 5 per cent. of the delegates had been members since before the civil war, and that, out of the 260,000 party
members in 1918, only 20,000 remained within the ranks."*

Similar changes have taken place in the governing structure of
the country. The original system of genuine soviets was replaced
by a mock soviet system where the organs which theoretically represented the workers were brought under the direct dominion of the
party. Then this in turn was replaced by the mock parliamentary
system of the 1936 constitution.

To-day, once again, Russia is going through a series of changes
in constitution, in political domination, in party organisation. In the
1936 Constitution, for instance, there was a clause guaranteeing
the workers a 7 hour day. This was never adhered to in practice,
and now there comes a change in wording which states that the
Russian workers are to work an 8 hour day, except in certain un-

*See *The Yogi and the Commissar,* by Arthur Koestler, London, 1945.

specified trades with hard conditions of work. In other words, even theoretically, the Russian workers will have to work a much longer week than the British or American workers seem likely to obtain in the near future. A second significant change is in the education clause of the Constitution. In the 1936 document it ran:

This right (of education) is ensured by universal compulsory elementary education, free of charge, including higher education, by the system of State stipends for the overwhelming majority of students in higher schools.

In the new document it runs:

This right is ensured through universal compulsory elementary education; free seven-year education; a system of State scholarships to pupils who distinguish themselves in higher schools.

This change is, of course, meant to cover up the fact that the recent education decrees, re-introducing fee-paying into high schools and universities, have been in direct contradiction to the 1936 constitution.

These changes in the constitution have been accomplished by widespread changes in the party organisation. During the past year there has been a steady purge of party organisations, as well as of various administrations throughout the country, on the alleged ground that counter-revolutionary attitudes have crept in—the old way of saying that during the crisis period following the war some people have been showing their independence rather too much for the authorities' liking.

At the head of affairs similar changes have taken place. During the war, the army leaders had great influence, and were continually in the limelight. Now they have been pushed into the background, and the lead is once more taken by the small group of men who form the Politburo, the real leading group of the party, and who also have within their power all the really important governmental posts.

The names of these men are, for the most part, not those of celebrated Bolsheviks, nor does there appear among them a single one of the generals who were so much glamorised in the last war. The actual names on the list are Stalin, Molotov, Beria, Zhdanov,

Voroshilov, Mikoyan, Malenkov, Kaganovitch, Andreyev, Khruschov, Zoznesensky, Bulganin, Kosygin and Shvernik. Only about four of these names are familiar to English readers, and many of them are not very well known to the Russians. They are, for the most part, ruthless administrators who have succeeded the old revolutionaries of the pre-1917 period, and who are without the least concern for anything but the efficient administration of their departments and the maintenance of the dictatorship. All of them are creatures of Stalin, and significantly, many of them made the grade as secret police organisers or heresy-hunters. Beria started as head of the Cheka in Transcaucasia, and is now in charge of all the "security services". Bulganin was an early organiser of the Cheka in Nijni Novgorod and Moscow. Kosygin gained a formidable reputation as a party purger and Trotskyist hunter. Kaganovitch carried out the— to Stalin—valuable task of crushing the opposition in the Ukraine.

But the changes go on continually in Russia, and no doubt these men in turn will have their ups and downs of power. But it would be rash to assume that such changes necessarily mean that the dictatorship is on its last legs. They mean that it is changing its organisation to suit different circumstances. But the one encouraging fact remains that humanity should, after thirty years, be so untrustworthy that purges are still the order of the day. All opposition groups have long been crushed, and yet, even in the party itself, unreliable elements continue to appear, and this fact encourages one to believe that, when the dictatorship becomes sufficiently corrupt and vitiated, there will be enough desire for liberty in people's minds to unseat it, just as Fascism in Italy was destroyed by the people after twenty years of power.

March, 1947.

40. STALIN'S CHRISTMAS BOX

IF WE can believe the *Daily Worker*, Stalin's Christmas present to the Russian people, the devaluation of the rouble and the abolition of rationing, will be received with jubilation. "At a single blow," says this newspaper admiringly,

"the Soviet Government has ended all rationing and restored peace-time trading, raised the purchasing power of the rouble, lowered the cost of living, maintained wages and deprived speculators of nine-tenths of their ill-gotten war-time gains."

It will have come as a shock for many to learn that there are such creatures as "spivs" in Russia. We had been led to understand that the black market was peculiar to our corrupted economic system, and that thanks to wise economic measures, Russia had not suffered from this curse.

Any black-marketeering which existed (if one can give it that name) was regulated by the Government and in fact most of it took place in State shops. It now appears, however, that there was another black market which forced the government to carry out a drastic currency reform.

We had also been told, Reg Bishop devoted a whole pamphlet to telling us,* that Soviet millionaires were not unscrupulous individuals like their capitalist counterparts, for: " . . . in the Soviet Union the millionaire has acquired his roubles by his own toil and by services to the Soviet State and People."

It seems rather unfair, in the light of this, that he should be deprived of part of his fortune. Let us see how this man, who has deserved so well of his country, would fare under the new decree. Let us take the case of that farmer, mentioned by Reg Bishop, who had managed to put aside one million roubles.

If the millionaire-farmer had by ill luck stuffed his money in his mattress he will now have to go to a bank and receive one rouble for ten of the old ones. If, on the other hand, he had put his money in a savings bank or State bank, his first 3,000 roubles will be changed at par. But if he had been wise enough to put it in a co-operative

Soviet Millionaires by Reg Bishop (Russia Today Society) London, 1944.

undertaking or a collective farm, he will receive four roubles for five.

In whatever way the wealthy farmer had invested the money, he will have to bear a substantial loss.

Let us consider the happier fate of a typical Russian factory worker. He earns 900 roubles a month and has managed to save 1,000 roubles to buy some clothes. He has no bank account, so he keeps his savings in his wallet; he will get a hundred roubles in exchange, but his loss will be insignificant compared with that of the farmer. As the decree points out the losses to the working people will be "short-termed and insignificant".

The *News Chronicle,* unlike the *Daily Worker* and the *Daily Express* did not comment enthusiastically on the new measures. Its City Editor described them as "an act of the purest *laissez-faire* economy" and remarked in a typical petit-bourgeois manner:

"Henceforth, apparently, the (Russia's) citizens will be able to buy food and clothing insofar as they have money to pay for them. That is the classic capitalist system, though it is now in full operation in comparatively few capitalist countries. In this respect the Communist wheel has come the full circle."

By one of those curious hazards of history it was announced that the United States were considering the introduction of food rationing practically at the same time as Russia announced that she was giving up hers. It conclusively shows how mistaken the city editor of the *News Chronicle* is in comparing Russian methods to those of capitalist countries.

With the abolition of rationing, the "commercial shops" where unrationed food was sold at a higher price, also disappear. We expressed some doubts, in the past, on the validity of this two-price system, from a Socialist view-point. Even Reg Bishop's able defence of this method did not convert us. Perhaps he will be more successful in explaining to us why these expensive shops, which, according to him existed for the benefit of the workers should have been abolished and why these same workers are expected to be pleased about it.

We should also like to know how the Russian worker can feel very elated because bread and macaroni have gone down in price when the price of milk, eggs, tea, fruit, clothes and footwear will be higher than the former rationed prices.

The abolition of clothes rationing is surprising in view of the shortage of consumer goods about which the Government has never made a secret. Their price was already much higher in relation to wages, than in Britain. But the remedy for these increases is hard work, longer hours resulting in a bigger wage packet, a solution which cannot have escaped the vigilant attention of the Government. Indeed, the *Daily Worker* might have mentioned that the "single blow" was administered with a double-edged weapon.

We feel compelled to mention one disturbing aspect of the introduction of this new decree. If Stalin was out to catch black-marketeers he should have seen that the secret was well kept. Instead, accurate forecasts appeared three weeks before the news was officially announced in the foreign press, and we learn that in Russia shops were emptied of their goods. If Dalton was forced to resign, what should be the fate of the Trotskyist-fascist who softened the "single blow"?

December, 1947.

41. COMMUNIST TERROR IN EASTERN EUROPE

THE CONTROL by Russia of countries generally described as being behind the "iron curtain" is even more ruthless than military occupation. The dirty work of repression is being done by native Communists, but the pattern according to which it is carried out has been imported from Moscow and is applied over and over again with a monotonous regularity.

The tactics used by the Communist Party have been described with particular acuteness by four American correspondents after they had completed an extensive tour of Eastern and Central Europe. The conquest of power is achieved in two movements:

1st Movement: Before Communists seize power outright, the correspondents noted that seven *vital conditions* are necessary: a Communist Minister of the interior to control the police, a Communist or pro-Communist Minister of Justice (courts), a Communist or "obedient" chief of staff (army), a Cabinet of Communists and others "willing or forced" to go along, a Parliament with a Communist controlled majority, non-Communist parties "intimidated and badgered", a Press censor under Communist orders.

2nd Movement: When the above conditions are obtained the Communists are ready to strike; they: "First—Accuse the opposition of plotting civil war, foreign (American) intervention, and economic sabotage . . . Second—Ban the opposition press . . . Third—Now go ahead and make your arrests . . . Fourth—Ban the most powerful opposition party . . . Fifth—Now stop and digest your gains. Hang the opposition chief . . . and your work is complete."

Though the chronological order might not always be rigorously observed the· pattern is fundamentally the same for every country. We have seen it applied in its last stages in Roumania and Bulgaria and we are seeing the first phase unfolding itself at present in Czechoslovakia.

The trials themselves are carried out according to a well-known pattern, as has been pointed out by a correspondent of the *Manchester Guardian* (4/11/47):

"It has been clear for some time that the numerous political trials that have taken place in Eastern Europe during the last couple of years have all followed closely a single pattern. It has been equally obvious where the original for this pattern was created. Apart from the striking similarity in the phraseology of the indictments and in the general conduct of these trials there is one specific charge, the intrinsic unlikeliness of which has not prevented its being preferred against the accused with a monotonous insistence. This is the charge of acting for, or receiving aid from, a foreign Power against the interests of the State. The foreign Power is invariably Britain or the United States, or both.

This charge was one of the central aspects of all the great Russian trials before the war. It was fundamental to the State prosecution's technique. For instance, it featured largely in the trials of Bukharin and the leading Trotskyists. They were said to be in touch with reactionary forces abroad. Though in all these cases much weight is given to that aspect which relates to activities of, or on behalf of, some foreign Power, the evidence adduced is invariably somewhat vague and indirect. Nor has the attention of the Government of the foreign Power mentioned ever been formally drawn to the alleged evidence connecting it, or its nationals, with the illegal activities of the accused. This step would seem normal if concern was really felt at the 'evidence'.

The bringing into these trials of the foreign threat is just part of the inevitable technique, or pattern, for their conduct. It has been found in Russia, since the days of Denikin, Kolchak, and Wrangel, that nothing so much provoked popular condemnation and hatred of a man as to charge him with working with foreign assistance against the people and the State."

In spite of the inexorability of the Communist conquest which always leads to a complete crushing of the opposition, this opposition has, in the first place, collaborated with the Communists and failed to oppose the framing of repressive legislation. Members of the socialist, liberal, agrarian parties have, at the beginning, nourished illusions as to their country's independence and have even strongly denied any interference from Moscow. Whether willing or unwilling tools, whether sincere or hypocritical, they have helped the Communists in the hope that they would save their skins by so doing.

By a stupid policy of compromise, these politicians have not only forfeited their positions, their freedom and lives, but have allowed hundreds of people to be arrested and judicially murdered. For each case which hits the headlines there are hundreds of obscure opponents who are imprisoned, sent to concentration camps, or killed. Our own comrades of the Bulgarian Anarchist Federation who have been amongst the most steadfast opponents of their country's long series of totalitarian régimes, have been rigorously suppressed.*

In Czechoslovakia the Communists have created the *vital conditions* which make their complete seizure of power necessary. They have the majority in the Czech parliament, they control the Ministries of the Interior, Information, Agriculture, Social Welfare; and the Prime Minister is a Communist. At the head of the Army they placed General Svoboda, commander of the Czech corps in Russia during the war and reputed to be a Communist.

In Slovakia, however, the Communists are in a minority and the machinery of plots and trials has been set in motion to transform this minority into a majority (the general elections are scheduled for next May, but the C.P. prefers not to have to rely on them). They have therefore:

1. Discovered a plot involving about 150 Slovaks and accused them of preparing an armed uprising and the assassination of President Benes.†

2. Deprived two Slovak M.P.s of their parliamentary immunity.

3. Arrested the Lord Mayor of Slovakia's capital, Bratislava, Dr. Josef Kysely, and Dr. Jan Kempny, former secretary of the Slovak Democratic Party.

4. Obtained the resignation of one of Czechoslovakia's deputy Prime Ministers, the Slovak Democrat Dr. Jan Ursiny.

5. As we go to press, the third secretary of the Democratic Party, Mr. Hodza, is expecting to be arrested (the two other secretaries are already in prison) and two Communist nominees are going to be appointed to the departments of Justice and the Interior in Slovakia.

Conclusion: Czechoslovakia will soon be ripe for a series of trials (with possible executions), the banning of newspapers and parties, and a régime of police terror.

November, 1947.

*See the "Appeal to Justice" manifesto in *Freedom*, 31/5/47.

†It is interesting to note that the former Communist leaders now on trial in Czechoslovakia are accused of plotting to assassinate Gottwald, Benes' successor as President.—EDITOR.

42. TERROR TRIALS IN JUGOSLAVIA†

THE COMMUNIST terror in Jugoslavia continues to follow the orthodox Russian pattern, with concentration camps, secret police and political trials which are conducted on a basis of fantasy that, if it were not combined with a barbarous ferocity, would verge on the comic. Any individuals or groups who oppose the régime, or attempt in any way to criticise the régime or to get out of the country information about atrocities committed by the authorities, are treated with the most ruthless brutality, and either disappear into the concentration camps or are made the victims of theatrically staged trials which slavishly imitate the Moscow purge trials in all their manifest injustice.

The most recent of these trials has been that of a number of Jehovah's Witnesses, who were accused of attempting to instigate a war against Jugoslavia, and of co-operating with reactionary groups to this end. This accusation seems quite incredible when one remembers the magnificent record of the Jehovah's Witnesses in their opposition to the recent war. We do not support the theocratic ideas of the members of this sect, but their heroic and consistent resistance to the Nazi terror in Germany cannot be denied, nor can the persecutions which they have endured in almost every country of the world during recent years for their opposition to war. Everywhere they have suffered really savage sentences of imprisonment rather than accept the dictates of the State to fight in wars which they did not support. Even in disagreement with their general views, one has to admit this consistency and disinterested courage.

It therefore seems self-evidently ridiculous to accuse such people of fomenting war on behalf of reactionary groups abroad, by which is presumably meant the British and American ruling classes who gave them savage sentences of imprisonment for their opposition to war!

The Jugoslav Embassy have recently issued an information bulletin on this case; it reads like the most hysterical Nazi or Communist apologetics for terrorist action under the guise of legality.

The document starts with a general accusation that the J.W.'s were—

"under the cloak of religious activities, connected with centres working to instigate a new war. They also enabled foreign reactionary groups to carry on activities liable to threaten our people and

†At the time when this article was written Russia and Jugoslavia were still allies.—EDITOR.

security and to undermine the democratic achievements (sic) of the national liberation struggle. The accused were instigating the severance of diplomatic relations and the abrogation of international treaties with the Federal People's Republic of Yugoslavia as well as interference in her internal affairs."

The specific activities of the J.W.'s appeared in the following paragraph which says that—

"under the guise of religious work (they) spread propaganda against People's Authorities of the Federal People's Republic of Yugoslavia. They persuaded their followers to shirk conscription, sent untrue reports on the political and economic situation of the country to international centres of their organisation in Berne and Brooklyn and in this way placed themselves directly at the service of international reactionaries."

In other words, the Jehovah's Witnesses held their own opinions instead of supporting Tito, they refused military service, and sent out of the country information which they considered should be known abroad. We know the old methods of Communist thought by which such activities are made to seem something very different from what they are in reality.

But even if the accusations—which accusations are supported by literally no evidence—are true, it is a singularly strange form of "democratic achievement" to sentence men to death because they happen to disagree with the Government of a country and endeavour to overthrow it. This is what happened to three of the accused in this trial. Eleven others were sentenced to various terms of imprisonment.

The case was immediately taken up by various English organisations as soon as the news came through, including the War Resisters' International, the Peace Pledge Union and the Freedom Defence Committee, and protests were sent to Jugoslavia *via* the Embassy. News has since come through that the sentences of death have been commuted to sentences of twenty years imprisonment.

But it is not enough to get a sentence of death by shooting merely changed to a long death in a Tito prison. Agitation must continue until the facts of such trials are sufficiently widely known for protests on a really wide international scale, to force the Jugoslav dictatorship to give up its victims.

March, 1947.

43.   UKRAINIAN WITCH HUNT

ALEXANDER WERTH, recently described by Walter Holmes, columnist of the *Daily Worker*, as a "reliable correspondent"* (a well-earned compliment considering that journalist's consistent efforts to white-wash the Russian régime), describes in the *Manchester Guardian* a purge carried out amongst Russian writers.   It bears a strange resemblance to the heresy hunt which has recently taken place in the United States.

Like Hollywood actors, Soviet writers seem to be prone to all kinds of deviations of which they are blissfully unaware but which do not escape the vigilant eye of the Board of the Ukrainian Writers' Union, a kind of Committee of un-Soviet Activities.   This Board has discovered that some Ukranian novelists, poets and critics were not doing their duty in promoting Communist ideals or the Soviet way of life.

According to the Ukranian Writers' Union, says Werth, some writers show "nationalist" trends.   Moreover, some poets, including the elderly Ukranian poet, Maxim Rylsky, still show escapist and "art for art's sake" tendencies:

"The well-known novelist Y. Yanovsky is severely attacked for his 'artistically and ideologically decadent' novel *Live Waters*.

'He has borrowed from reactionary literature the idea that things biological, instinctive, and animal are superior to things rational, social, and human.   These bourgeois-decadent conceptions are applied to the description of Soviet people and of the post-war collective farms in the Ukraine.   Among Yanovsky's people the majority are morally decadent people, or sadists, like one of his Ukrainian characters, Gandzi, who, during the Occuption, "astonished even the Germans by his cruelty" . . .   His world is dominated by cruelty and pathological passions.'

Another writer, I. Senchenko, is accused of having written a 'slanderous' novel, *Our Generation,* 'containing a lampoon of Soviet youth.'   These people are guilty of having, 'under the guise of nationalist romanticism, put across a pessimistic bourgeoise philosophy of life and mankind.   Such an approach to life can only condemn literature to a slavish dependence on the West and to complete decay.'

*Alexander Werth is no longer *persona grata* in the Communist Press.   His sympathies appear to lie more with the Tito régime.—EDITOR.

Maxim Rylsky is particularly attacked for an 'escapist' poem, *Journey into my Youth.*"

What Mr. Werth is in a better position than we are to find out is why so many writers produce "escapist" literature. There should be no desire to escape, if only with a poem, from a workers' (and writers') paradise.

Mr. Werth's only comment is that the line taken by the Ukrainian Writers' Union "is, *of course*, (italics ours) completely consistent with the line taken in Russia proper". And to prove that the "line" never wavers he tells us how in Russia two writers were selected by Zhdanov, in his famous address, as examples of the "wrong point of view": Anna Akhmatova, "who was said to be an escapist, largely living sentimentally in the past and absorbed in her personal emotions and Zoschenwo, who was described as trivial, frivolous and cynical in his distorted portrayal of Soviet life".

Again, like some Hollywood actors, Soviet writers know on which side their bread is buttered and can take a hint. "Zoschenko," Werth tells us, "has shown signs of mending his ways and a recent number of *Novy Mir*, publishes humorous 'sketches' of life among the partisans of the Leningrad province, with ludicrous Germans as the chief source of merriment. Now he is also writing a comic play called *How I Became an American Millionaire*—which is sure to be a success!"

The late Reg Bishop told us how one became a Soviet Millionaire. We have done our best to give publicity to his pamphlet which achieved only a small part of the success it deserved.

January, 1948.

44. MORE SABOTAGE IN RUSSIA?

WE HAVE been repeatedly told that Russia got rid of its fifth column long ago. It was a tough job and apart from the people shot or otherwise "eliminated", millions of people have been put in concentration camps.

David Y. Dallin and Boris Nicolaevsky, authors of *Forced Labour in Soviet Russia,* relying on official Soviet sources, estimate that the number of people in slave labour camps has varied from 7 to 12 millions. This statement has brought on them all the fury of Mr. Vishinsky who, before a committee of the United Nations, described them as "idiots or gangsters" who got their information from "Hitlerite agents".

Unabashed, Dallin and Nicolaevsky are seeking to institute a $1,000,000 slander suit against Andrei Vishinsky and their counsel has asked Mr. Vishinsky to waive his diplomatic immunity and accept service of the complaint, so that the issues involved can be tried before an impartial American court.

It is unlikely that anybody will be able to establish the exact number of prisoners in Russia. Only the overthrow of Stalin's régime may bring to light the many times duplicated records of the N.K.V.D.

Whether there are seven or twelve million prisoners, one thing appears certain and it is that all the "saboteurs", "fascist agents", etc., have not yet been rounded up. They seem particularly active just now in sabotaging the turn-round of railway wagons.

The State Prosecutor's office has issued a statement, which was broadcast (presumably by way of encouraging the others) giving details of sentences passed by military tribunals between October and December on railway officials who had "systematically allowed delays in loading and unloading goods wagons at stations and industrial undertakings."

We can only give two examples of these sentences (quoted more extensively in the *Manchester Guardian,* 8/1/48):

"M. V. Bulgakov, head of the Argamach mine, Eletsk Mining Board: Two years' 'deprivation of liberty', for having allowed 13,300 wagon-hours to be lost at night and on days off when wagons had stood idle (sentence passed by Moscow-Donbas Railway Military Tribunal on November 28);

L. K. Groman, head of the Lenin section, Topstroymontazh

Trust, Ministry of Fuel Enterprises Construction: Three years' 'deprivation of liberty', for having caused the loss of 11,050 wagon-hours, through failure to use unloading machines to full capacity and failure to supply workers with the necessary tools (sentence passed by the Tomsk Railway Military Tribunal on October 6)."

The severity of the sentences by military courts, the use of the word *systematically* in the State Prosecutor's statement clearly show that the condemned officials are treated like saboteurs, wilfully trying to undermine the State.

Either these men are not guilty of systematically allowing delays, etc., and in that case it is a sad reflection on Soviet Justice that they should be condemned, or they are guilty, and it shows that thirty years after the revolution and after more than twenty years of continuous purges Stalin's régime does not command the loyalty of the citizens.

January, 1948.

45. FROM THE HORSE'S MOUTH

THE AMERICAN *New Leader* tells us of a new trick American plutocrats have got up to:

"Vishinsky should take note that the Fascists, Social Fascists, Trotskyites and other agents of Wall Street have developed a new especially dangerous method of anti-Soviet propaganda. They simply take books, magazine articles, and other sources of Communist wisdom, translate them word by word into English, and present them to the American public.

This vile trick was perpetrated recently when the *Modern Review* translated from the magazine *Bolshevik,* M. Dynnik's article on Contemporary Bourgeois Philosophy in the U.S.A. And now a book has been published called *I Want To Be Like Stalin,* which reproduces the chapters on moral and civic education from an official pedagogical textbook, published in Russia in 1946. The book has a very able and very moderate introduction by George S. Counts, who chose the texts and translated them together with Mucia P. Lodge. But the 'real thing' is the Russian text itself."

And to think there was a time when American publishers decided not to publish, and even withdrew from circulation, books critical of Russia!

January, 1948.

46. THE MYTH OF CZECH DEMOCRACY

WE ARE getting used to the creation of myths. At one time we only had a Russian myth, now we have a Polish myth, an Eastern Zone of Germany myth, a Hungarian myth. The most popular, however, seems to be the Czech myth. According to fellow-travellers of Tom Driberg's type,* we have much to learn from this model democracy which is wrongly being accused of hiding behind an iron curtain.

That the country is dominated by the Communists seemed to me obvious during my short stay in Czechoslovakia. Nobody seems to have any doubts about it in the country itself and they would be surprised to read the accounts of British journalists who claim that Czechoslovakia is free from any party's domination and foreign interference. No doubt these journalists have not met, as I did, people who have been imprisoned for months without any reason being given; people who have been interrogated by the secret police for alleged criticisms of the Communist Party. Some of these journalists were in Czechoslovakia at the time, or soon after the arrest and brutal treatment of *Illustrated*'s correspondents, yet none of them mention the incident and they talk gaily about the freedom of the Press. None of them seem to have seen German prisoners employed as slave labour on the land. None of these brilliant and inquiring-minded journalists has apparently bothered to find out who were the women prisoners working in the fields, dressed in patched trousers made of camouflage material and wearing torn shirts. None of them has asked why they were there, what they had done, if they received any pay or when they will be returned to their families.

We hear, however, all kinds of generalisations as to Czechoslovakia's democratic régime and complete independence. How do these stand up to the facts?

Francis Lint, writing in *World Review,* Oct. 1947, asserts: "There has, till now, been no evident interference with Czechoslovakia's external and internal affairs."

This was written two months after we had seen the most glaring example of Russia's interference in Czechoslovakia's foreign policy regarding the Marshall Plan. On July 9th, the Czechoslovak Gov-

*Mr. Tom Driberg is no longer *persona grata* with the Communists and *vice versa.*—EDITOR.

ernment announced that it would go to Paris to discuss the Marshall Plan. A few hours later this decision was suddenly reversed. How could a decision, reached unanimously by the four parties in the Government: Communist, National Socialist, Social Democratic and People's Catholic Party, be reversed so rapidly?

Worldover Press (New York) in its bulletin 12-19th September, gives a detailed analysis of the reasons for this *volte-face*. It points out that the first decision was mainly dictated by economic reasons, the second was political and dictated by Stalin's foreign policy.

Czechoslovakia's economy depends on the West and can only with difficulty be geared to that of Russia.

"Even in February, 1947," *Worldover Press* points out, "when Czech exports to Russia reached their peak, they were no more than seven per cent. of the total exports. In August of this year, one of the largest orders was delivered to Russia: 10,000,000 Czech crowns (£50,000) worth of lathes. But such an order is exceptional. On the whole Czechoslovak industry cannot meet Soviet needs.

For example, the most important industrial production in Czechoslovakia is that of fine, specialized glass: cut glass, optical and art glass including the recently developed etched glass. But there is no demand for such things in Russia. On the other hand, they are more and more in demand in all Western countries.

Or take the shoe industry. All of it, including the now nationalized Bata works, produces high-quality goods so expensive that few Czechs can afford to buy them. Most of these shoes are destined for foreign markets and are an important item in paying for the raw materials the country needs most. Very few of these shoes find their way to Russia. As a member of the Soviet trade delegation put it, 'We do not need such playthings'. What the Russians need are heavy-duty, country boots, and their feet, moreover, are generally larger than those of the Czechs. The first consignment of shoes to the U.S.S.R. has been returned for that reason, and not much has been done since.

The newspapers gloss over the fact that even to-day Czechoslovakia has a greater trade with occupied Germany than with Russia. But they play up every shipment of goods to Russia, and whenever the Soviet Union sends something to Czechoslovakia the, Czech papers announce it loudly with such headlines as 'Russia Meets Her Obligations'."

The article quoted above explains that the very day on which Prague announced that Czechoslovakia would take part in the Paris conference, Stalin received Gottwald, the Communist Prime Minister and other Czech delegates to discuss the political implications of a treaty of alliance with France. This question, however, was left aside and Stalin instead asked the Czech Government to stay away from Paris. Gottwald reported this talk by phone to his colleagues in Prague and at a secret session, in spite of the opposition of some members, the Czech Government reversed their previous decision.

This policy was justified on the grounds that Czechoslovakia could not afford to cut herself off from the East as, in case of a new German aggression, no country but Russia was certain to come to her rescue.

At the elections in May, 1946, the Communists polled 38 per cent. of all votes, which made them the largest party in the country. The Communist success was due in great part to the rôle played by Russia in the liberation of the country (although it is generally believed that if the Americans stopped before Prague and waited for five days for the Red Army to liberate the capital it was because of an understanding between the Allied High Commands).

Another reason, according to Francis Lint, is that many "voted Communist because, having become members of the Party at a time when it was generally assumed they would grab power under the shadow of Russian bayonets, they were interested in a Communist victory to secure their positions."

The Government is a coalition in which the Communists hold the key ministries: the Prime Minister is a Communist and the Ministry of the Interior, which controls the police, the Ministry of Information which controls the State-owned radio, the film industry and paper supplies, the Ministries of Agriculture and Social Welfare, are all in the hands of the Communist Party.

The Communists only obtained the majority of votes among the Czechs; in Slovakia they are in a minority, having obtained 21 seats while the Slovak Democrats obtained 43. But even in Slovakia the Communists are holding the Ministry of Interior with the police.

Slovakia has proved refractory to Communist propaganda. 'Slovaks' aim at greater autonomy, having little in common with the Czechs. They have a shadow cabinet in Bratislava but Ministries of War, Finance and Foreign Affairs are centralised in Prague. Unable to get the support of the Slovak population the Communist Party has begun a conversion by force, according to the well-known pattern.

A plot has been discovered in Slovakia and the Communist Minister of the Interior, Vaclav Nosek, has asked Parliament to suspend the immunity of two M.P.s, belonging to the Slovak Democratic Party, accused of being involved in the plot. *News Review* dryly comments: "It is a neat move. The Slovak Democrats have 43 members in the Czechoslovak Parliament, 43 minus two is 41. This sort of arithmetic did wonders in Hungary. It brings Gottwald a little nearer his majority."

Stalin can withdraw his Red Army from Central Europe with a light heart. By the time the last Russian soldier has left, most of the opposition will be in jail, shot or hanged.

Tourists are given a booklet to guide them during their Czechoslovak holiday. It explains concisely what "freedom of the Press" means in that country: "The Press has been reorganised and no newspaper may be privately owned. All papers and periodicals have to be published, under licence of the Czechoslovak Ministry of Information, by Political Parties or approved cultural or professional associations. Beyond this there is no censorship of the Press."

Further censorship is understandably enough unnecessary; the Minister of Information is a Communist.

How free journalists are in Czechoslovakia, has been discovered the hard way by cameraman Erich Auerbach and Jack Winocour, of the British weekly *Illustrated,* who went to Czechoslovakia last month, at the invitation of the Czech Ministry of Foreign Affairs. They received assurances from various ministers that they would have complete freedom for their work. "If you run into any iron curtain, come and tell us," they were told jokingly.

As it happened they did run into it, but when they tried to tell the ministers about it all they were met with were insults and threats. While visiting Slovakia they were arrested, manhandled and assaulted by the State Security Police, their camera and films confiscated. They do not know to this day the reason for this treatment and for the fine which they were given under a Fascist law which is still in force. They were only released after the intervention of the British Consul.

This could be dismissed as the irresponsible action of stupid and brutal policemen if apologies or explanations had been offered them at their release. Instead they found an hostile attitude in the ministers who had warmly welcomed them on their arrival, and the Ministry of the Interior, when returning the negatives, used threatening language and warned them that they were liable to five years' imprisonment. The Press completely distorted the incident. I was in Czechoslovakia at the time and from the Communist newspapers one got the impression that the two British correspondents had assaulted frontier guards!

The Ministers responsible for this incident are: the Slovak Minister of Interior (Communist), the Czech Minister of Interior (Communist), the Minister of Information (Communist)—in other words, the people who laugh loudest when the words "iron curtain" are mentioned.

We are told that Czechoslovakia's politics are governed by fear and distrust of Germany. Inside the country it manifested itself by the expulsion of 3 million Germans (one-fifth of the population) and the confiscation of their property. The justification for this inhuman policy is to be found, apparently, in the sufferings undergone by the Czechs under the German occupation.

This explanation seems particularly startling when one hears it on arriving in Czechoslovakia after having crossed Germany. After seeing a devastated, half-starved country, Czechoslovakia, where there is hardly any trace of bombing, and where people are well-fed and dressed, seems almost unreal. They have suffered through Hitler but the German people are paying more dearly for his crimes.

One does not wish to underestimate the sufferings of the Czechs under German occupation but if sufferings inevitably breed hatred many other European countries would have far greater reasons to hate the Germans. Yet nowhere in Europe has hatred manifested itself in such a violent, base, petty manner. It would certainly never have assumed such a character had it not been exacerbated for political and economic reasons.

The expulsion of three million Germans deprived Czechoslovakia of valuable manpower but the property of these people was transferred to Czechs. To expel Germans meant that there was a possibility of acquiring a shop, a farm, or some other property for nothing. According to Francis Lint, who tries to justify this policy:

"Driving out these Germans, turning these regions into Czech districts and repopulating them was a hard task. In the beginning people flocked in their thousands into the border regions. When it became known, however, that nobody could be certain of owning the farm, the house, the shop, he had taken over, when it became clear that the Government considered them only as some sort of 'national caretakers' the situation became difficult. A lot of adventurers just sucked dry what they had taken over, and left before they were found out. Others, qualified and honest citizens who really wanted to make a new start, became disgusted when the Government put off the decision to hand the properties over to private ownership. This state of affairs led for a short time to re-emigration into the interior, but the Government has realised its error and all properties are shortly to be handed over to their present holders."

If the German occupation disorganised State finances, it left, on the other hand, many new factories, such as, for example, the refineries for synthetic oil in North-Western Bohemia which produce enough synthetic oil to meet the whole country's petrol consumption. This mammoth works, says Lint, "has been named 'Stalin's Works', as a token of gratitude to the Russians who did not confiscate it as war booty but handed it over as a gift to the Czechoslovak Government" (French people never thought of renaming the Renault works after Churchill or Roosevelt!).

As far as Slovakia was concerned she seemed to have prospered economically during the war, being for a long time Germany's hinterland.

All this cannot and should not be put against the executions, arrests and deportations carried out by the Nazis, but one is obliged to remember these facts when Czechoslovakia is represented as Germany's victim *par excellence*. They also lead one to believe that the hatred of Germany has been, to a considerable extent, fostered to serve political ends.

To keep Czechoslovakia under Russia's influence the Communist Party must encourage the fear of Germany and, at the same time, the distrust of the Western Powers.   To this end they must hide these elementary truths:

(a) To hate Germans as a nation is contrary to every principle of socialism—a distinction must be made between the Nazis and the ordinary German people.

(b) Chamberlain's Munich which the Czechs can neither forget nor forgive was followed by Molotov's Munich which might have prevented their liberation for years to come.

(c) When Spain was fighting alone against Fascism did Czecho-slovakia, which possessed one of the finest air forces of Europe send any help?

(d) Russia has clearly demonstrated that she has no respect for the independence of small states (Baltic States, Poland, etc.).   If the Czechs are so concerned with their national independence, it is ridiculous for them to fear a defeated Germany and yet trust Russia's power.

Fear of Germany, distrust of Britain and America, hopes of Russian protection will only lead the Czech people to new and probably greater sufferings.   Their allies are the workers of other countries, whether in Germany, Britain or Russia.   Together they can struggle for a common aim of freedom and peace.

November, 1947.

47.   GUILTY MEN IN PRAGUE

As COMMUNIST shock-troops parade in Prague, the cold war shows signs of warming up.   In less than ten years Czechoslovakia, hailed as a paragon of democracy, has fallen under a totalitarian rule without opposing any considerable resistance.

Unlike the great majority of the British Press and apparently even our Foreign Office, we cannot pretend to be surprised or shocked by the Communist seizure of power.   Czechoslovakia has been under virtual Communist domination ever since the Red Army walked through the streets of Prague for purposes of "liberation".   This dramatic show of Russian power was carried out with the consent of the Allies.   What has taken place since—a gradual and systematic consolidation of Communist control—has been watched in silence by the "great democracies".

Up to a few months ago most of the articles about Czechoslovakia which appeared in the British Press claimed that it was a true democracy, that freedom of speech and of the Press were respected, that Benes and Masaryk were great democrats who knew how to preserve the independence of their country.   And yet now that the showdown has taken place we see that these great statesmen have acted little better than quislings.   Benes has accepted the new government, which has thereby been formed in "a constitutional manner"; Masaryk has retained his post of Foreign Minister, and then conveniently retired to the country with an illness which made him speechless.

The Communists are very anxious to demonstrate that everything in Czechoslovakia has been carried out in the most constitutional way.   The Communist Party, they say, is the largest single party in the country.   What, then, is more natural than that it should have a little say in the affairs of the country?   It is strange, however, that it could not wait until the elections, which are to be held in May, to get things right.   In forcing the election issue it lays itself open to the suspicion that it was afraid of getting less votes than at the last elections, and that it was safer to seize power by force, disguised or otherwise.

To assert, as the *Daily Worker* does, that it was thanks to the militant action of the Czech workers that the government was changed is a huge joke.   To marvel, as the British Press and even diplomats (according to the *Sunday Times*) have done, at the swiftness with which the putsch was carried out, is to forget the trend of events in Czechoslovakia during the past few months.   What has happened during the past week is merely the logical outcome of a systematic infiltration by Russia.

In October, 1947, the Communist Party began to unearth plots against the Government, a sure prelude to the seizure of power.   They struck the first blow in Slovakia, where the Communist Party was in a minority.   They arrested about 150 Slovaks and accused them of preparing an armed uprising, and, curiously, the assassination of President Benes (presumably they thought public opinion would feel more indignant at the projected assassination of a democrat than that of Communist Premier Gottwald).   They arrested leaders of the Slovak Democratic Party and obtained the resignation of Czechoslovakia's Deputy Prime Minister, Dr. Jan Ursiny.

This was followed by the discovery of a series of plots in Bohemia, and by widespread arrests. When it is remembered that the Communist Party controlled the Ministries of Interior, Information, Agriculture and Social Welfare, that the Prime Minister was a Communist, and that he had placed at the head of the army General Svoboda, who was commander-in-chief of the Czech corps in Russia during the war and reputed to be a Communist, it will be seen that the vital conditions for seizure of power had been created, and, as we wrote last November: "Czechoslovakia will soon be ripe for a series of trials (with possible executions), the banning of newspapers and parties, and a régime of police terror."

Thanks to the collaboration of Dr. Benes, the Communist Party was able to seize power with little show of violence, and the *Daily Worker* proudly announced that "Czechoslovakia has passed through the second phase of her national revolution without the loss of a single citizen's life". But the Communist Party will not be cheated out of a full-scale purge. The Communist-controlled Czech Central Action Committee has already issued a warning that decisions of the National Front will be binding on all, and that "it was absolutely necessary to purge the political parties of the enemies of popular democracy". Many members of the National Socialist Party have been arrested; in short, Czechoslovakia has gone the way of Roumania, Hungary and Poland.

Police measures have left Mr. Gottwald time to announce that all private enterprises employing over 50 people would be taken over by the State, and the splitting up of estates of over 125 acres would begin at once. This, it is hoped, will gain the Government some popular support, as the Prime Minister has enphasised that he does not wish to introduce collective farming: "In future, when someone whispers something like this to you, chase him out of the village," he said, addressing a meeting of farmers. Thus, we shall have the creation of kulaks, and Communist enthusiasts who would wish to establish in Czechoslovakia the wonderful system of collectivisation which exists in Russia will be "chased out of the village". But this, we like to believe, is only a phase in the dialectical process: When the kulaks have settled down they will be eliminated "as a class", as they were in Russia.

Russia has now established political and economic domination over seven countries with a population of 90 millions, and her appetite shows no signs of being satisfied. Having carried out her job in Prague with remarkable efficiency, Russia turned her interest to Finland where the forthcoming elections are expected to show a drop in the Communist vote and where, therefore, swift action may be necessary.

Austria is also beginning to feel distinctly uncomfortable, caught between Russia and Yugoslavia. In the general elections of 1945, the Austrian communist candidates won only four of the 165 electoral districts. The behaviour of Red Army troops does not seem to have won the effection of Austrians for communism. But here also this may be one more reason for acting quickly. Russia is applying strong economic and political pressure on Austria, while Tito has launched a full-scale propaganda campaign in Slovene territory and in other parts of Austria.

The iron curtain shows itself to be extremely elastic.

How helpless the "democratic" powers look in these events! They shout "murder", "rape", when Czechoslovakia falls a victim to totalitarianism. They sadly remember Munich, and feel as helpless to check Stalin as they did to check Hitler. If Britain finds itself at war with Russia in the near future, the government now in power will be blamed for having stood by while the "rape" and the "murder" were carried out. Yet what could the democracies do to prevent them, short of going to war with Russia?

It is a sinister reflection on democracy that her only victories are won thanks to machine guns, planes and atom bombs. The victory of totalitarianism in Czechoslovakia is not only a measure of Russia's strength; it is also a demonstration of the weakness and ineffectuality of democratic governments.

March, 1948.

48. CLEARING UP IN PRAGUE

EXACTLY A fortnight had passed between the beginning of the Czech crisis and the first meeting of the Communist dominated cabinet at which Mr. Gottwald, the Prime Minister, declared, rubbing his hands: "To-day we are sitting at a clean table in a ventilated room."

The "ventilation" has assumed the proportions of a tornado. Parliament is now safely in the hands of Communists. M.P.'s had been asked to sign the declaration of loyalty to the new Government before taking their seats; some had resigned and others were waiting the results of the investigation by their Party Parliamentary Committee.

Politicians had been arrested including Mr. Vladimir Krajna, secretary-general of the National Socialist Party, and Mr. Ota Hora and Mr. Alois Cizek, both National-Socialist Members of Parliament. A warrant of arrest was issued for Mr. Vaclav Majer, until recently the Social Democrat Minister for Food.

The cleaning-up extended outside political circles. The rector of the University of Prague and a score of professors were dismissed; judges, editors, and teachers are being purged and, Nejedly, the new Minister of Education, declared "Stalin's picture will return to the classrooms. This is not merely a matter of a picture, but a conception of national life". One could not agree more.

The Action Committee, now numbering 10,000 are carrying out the purge along the lines of General Svoboda's threatening directive: "Anyone who violates unity and refuses to co-operate is harmful to the nation and must be eliminated. It is necessary to destroy as quickly as possible and ruthlessly all elements of disruption and to finish what we have to finish."

Action Committees, the purging organs of the Communist Party, have sprung up everywhere: in factories, universities, Government offices, the radio and the Press. Even football players and Boy Scouts have their Action Committees. Their aim is to carry out the suppression of every dissident and a large campaign of denunciation is encouraged for this purpose. Secondary school children have been asked, over the radio, to name their fellow-pupils "hostile to the régime of a people's democracy, Socialism, and youth unity", as well as teachers "who are either unable or unwilling to teach".

What remained of a free press has been suppressed by with-holding power and paper supplies from newspapers "opposing the people's democracy". The socialist paper *Svobodne Slovo* (meaning Free World) has appropriately changed its title to *Nova Politika* (New Politics). Foreign publications have, of course, been banned.

The only safe place, for the time being at least, seems to be inside the Communist Party and new members are reported to be joining at the rate of over 2,000 a day. The aim is still two million members and it will no doubt be reached, as refusal to fill in application forms often means losing one's job.

The "democracies" pretend to be greatly shocked by these events but they find nothing better, to answer them, than to emulate the Czech Communists in their repression of freedom.

At the Hague, the Minister of Justice announced that a new police force would be created to combat the activities of Right-wing and Left-wing elements. The Swiss National Assembly called for increased vigilance by the Government against Communists and demanded that it should "strengthen regulations for the protection of the State." In the Ruhr, the British Military Government suppressed the last Communist paper still in existence.

We are not suggesting that the "democracies" are carrying out a repression of a magnitude and ruthlessness comparable with what is happening in Czechoslovakia. But one must remember that they are in power and that the opposition is extremely weak while the Czech Communists had to seize power in the face of considerable opposition.

If the democratic governments are showing such readiness to employ totalitarian measures when they are still in a comparatively secure position, as in the U.S.A. and in Canada in particular, will they not become as ruthless as the Czech Government if the opposition assumes greater proportions? Just as, in order to fight the Nazis, the democracies resorted to methods similar to those employed by Hitler, now, in the struggle against Communism, they adopt totalitarian measures which Stalin would not disavow.

March, 1948.

49. 'OUR DEAR JAN'

A BANKER who committed suicide during the inflation in Germany
remarked before his death: "A single corpse can move public opinion
but masses of corpses are merely statistics."

Because of this human idiosyncracy the death of Jan Masaryk
has succeeded in shaking the world, which had remained almost indifferent to the thousands of arrests and executions that have taken
place in Central Europe during the past year. According to a newspaper correspondent, his death has achieved a unity in the American
Press unknown since Pearl Harbour.

It is a bitter irony that the man who gave the example of collaboration with the Communists, who liked to think of himself as a
"bridge" between the West and Russia, who jovially assured everyone
that it was possible to compromise and yet retain one's freedom,
should have fallen the victim of his collaboration and that his death
should widen the gulf between East and West even more effectively
than Mr. Gottwald's putsch.

It took the Czech Government six hours to think up an explanation for Masaryk's death and it showed a certain ingenuity: Masaryk
was the victim of the democracies and in particular of his friends
abroad who had failed to appreciate his patriotic stand and had
deluged him with telegrams expressing their disapproval. With flowers,
orations and tears, the Communist leaders expressed their sorrow at
the death of a faithful friend.

But Masaryk's friends abroad refused to believe that he had
committed suicide, and if one is to believe them, Mr. Gottwald's
funeral oration assumes a sinister meaning: 'I must accompany our
dear Jan on his last trip" would mean that he had 'taken him for a
ride'. One does not need to be gifted with particular powers of
detection to notice a few contradictions in the official explanation of
his death. Mr. Gottwald claims that Masaryk from the first days of
the crisis "fully and spontaneously agreed with the action programme
of the new Government". From Masaryk's statements, prior to the
crisis, the most that can be said is, in fact, that he was dragged along
to support the new government.

The statement issued by the Czech Prime Minister's office is
equally unconvincing. The first paragraph states: "Mr. Jan Masaryk,

the Minister for Foreign Affairs, put an end to his life, devoted to the work of the nation and the country, as a result of his illness combined with insomnia. It is probable that in a moment of nervous disturbance he decided to end his life." But the second paragraph goes on to say: "Neither on the day before his tragic death nor yesterday evening did Mr. Masaryk show any signs of mental depression. On the contrary, he was full of life and of his usual optimism."

Those who favour the murder explanation believe that Masaryk had been prevented from expressing his disapproval of the new régime by the virtual imprisonment to which he had been subjected, but that he would have come out into the open when the Czech Parliament met for the first time since the crisis, on the day of his death. It was therefore necessary to eliminate him before he had a chance to speak.

A *Manchester Guardian* correspondent declares: "The possibility that it was not suicide cannot be dismissed; nor should one forget the comparison with the former Minister of Justice, Dr. Drtina, who was found injured in similar circumstances, but who, according to eye-witness accounts, was assaulted in the streets and then abandoned beneath the window of his flat.

The *Daily Worker,* on the other hand, shows a certain impatience towards those who claim that totalitarianism breeds death, suicides, assassinations, murders and executions. The *Daily Worker* is not in favour of making too much fuss over peoples' deaths and innocently remarks: "When John Winant committed suicide last November, it was explained that he was a man of deep conviction who suffered from overwork and bad health. There was no attempt politically to exploit his death." This is unimpeachable logic and it is quite true that the Communist Press never accused Mr. Truman of having hired a gunman to shoot Mr. Winant. Why cannot similar discretion be used in the case of Jan Masaryk?

Whether we shall ever know how Masaryk died, at least we know already that the most shameful use is going to be made of his memory. Mr. Gottwald's tears for his "dear Jan" are hardly more hypocritical than those of British, American and French politicians, who try to represent him as an "apostle of liberty" forgetting that for months before the crisis occurred, when it cannot be said that he had no opportunity to make his voice heard, he remained silent though people were being arrested whom he must have known to be innocent. They also forget that he retained his post as Foreign Minister in the present Government, thereby giving his consent, willingly or unwillingly, to it. His responsibility is all the greater because he (like Benes) had the reputation of being a real democrat. The Communist Party was able to make great play of their collaboration.

We do not intend to dispute Masaryk's corpse either with the Communists or with the democrats. He belonged to the line of "well-meaning" politicians who have always led the people to disaster. It was men of his stamp who allowed Mussolini to seize power; it was they who in the Weimar Republic opened the way to Hitler; it was they who refused to arm the Spanish workers when Franco's troops attempted to seize power. "Well-meaning" politicians spell the doom of the people as surely as bare-faced dictators. Jan Masaryk is dead but the sufferings of the Czech people have just begun.

March, 1948.

50. MARSHALL'S MIRACLE

THE AMERICAN State Department's report which gives estimates of the food, raw materials and machinery that will be shipped by the United States under the Marshall Plan, if Congress gives its approval, has sharpened the controversy as to the merits, or otherwise, of this scheme.

Mr. Truman and his associates have candidly presented the scheme as an essential instrument of American foreign policy and seem certain that it can "achieve miraculous results". The British Labour Party has now unreservedly rallied to these views and has called a European Congress of the Socialist parties in countries adhering to the Marshall Plan to be held in March. But the Beaverbrook Press and the Communist Party oppose the Plan as undermining Britain's independence, while claiming that they are not opposed to American aid.

On one point, however, there is general agreement, from Mr. Truman to Mr. Pollitt—that the Marshall Plan is being used as a political weapon. The issues become less clear when the economic aspects of the Plan are being discussed.

The United States would like the world to think of the Plan as a crusade against police States, totalitarian rule, political and moral chaos. They have abandoned the rôle of the philanthropist assumed at the beginning and taken up that of the crusader. There is a third rôle which they could play with little effort, but which is deprived of glamour, that of the business man. A 20th century business man, of course, who has mastered the art of buying the right kind of machinery and who is more fond of waving the torch of liberty than his cheque book. A 20th century business man who becomes a Tom Paine when the business rival is Stalin and who remains a plain business man when the customer is Peron.

The Marshall Plan is not, as it has often been described, an "example of a responsible and unselfish action". The Marshall Plan is business and as such it is outside ethical considerations. It can only be good or bad business, and the report, recently published, seems to indicate that it is not bad business.

It would be ridiculous, of course, to believe that America is merely trying to get rid of her surplus production. The plan will mean "sacrifices" which have been accepted all the more readily because it is understood that they will fall on the shoulders of the American worker rather than on those of the capitalists.

One can also see at a glance that the plan for future European recovery is going to mean the immediate recovery of certain American industries. Originally, the Marshall Plan was to provide (on a credit arrangement) bread for the workers and raw materials and plant equipment for industry. Now, very substantial trimmings have been added. The biggest item of the exports to Britain is tobacco and France and Switzerland are also to receive considerable quantities although they have not asked for it. It will neither feed nor give labour to European workers but it will help the badly hit American tobacco industry.

It is also difficult to understand how an "unselfish" administration could propose to increase American shipping construction by 34 million dollars during the next fiscal year, while suggesting that shipbuilding in Europe should be curtailed during the next four years.

It is a truism to say that the Marshall Plan will render Western Europe politically and economically subservient to the United States. The only two alternatives which have been put forward are that of the Beaverbrook Press, which demands greater efforts and sacrifices on the part of the workers (while advocating at the same time the re-introduction of the basic petrol ration to show clearly that the workers alone should not make sacrifices) and that of the Communist Party, which would like to replace the Marshall Plan by a Molotov Plan.

These two plans being obviously incompatible, Europe is being divided in two sections which should, rationally, complement each other. Before the war more than 60 per cent. of the total imports of countries now behind the iron curtain came from Western Europe while only about 15 per cent. came from Russia. These countries, on the other hand, were exporting many of the agricultural products and raw materials which the countries in the Marshall area must now import from America. As if frontiers were not bad enough, we now have iron curtains, dollar areas, sterling areas, etc. It is impossible for Europe to achieve a healthy economy until these artificial barriers disappear.

We cannot accept the Marshall Plan any more than we can accept capitalism and imperialism. We cannot support a Molotov plan any more than we can support totalitarianism. We refuse to take sides. One does not choose between the plague and cholera, particularly when one does not believe in miracles.

January, 1948.

51. DOES BRITAIN SHOW THE WAY?

DEMAGOGUES ARE always willing to take any excuse for changing a propaganda line that has worn itself out, and for Attlee the New Year was as good as anything else. Realising that the workers in Britain are becoming disgusted with both the American and the Russian régimes and are not inclined to be led away into support of either of them, he turned his New Year message into an attempt to represent "Socialist" Britain as being a third camp which alone shows the right way for the world to follow in its pursuit of social justice. Britain and the countries of Western Europe, he claims, are not "in any sense 'watered-down capitalism' or 'watered-down Communism'," but something quite different from either, and, adopting a Solomon-like attitude of self-righteousness, he condemns Russia for its lack of political freedom and America for basing its economy on capitalism.

It is true enough to say that "The history of Soviet Russia provides us with a warning here—a warning that, without political freedom, collectivism can quickly go astray and lead to new forms of oppression and injustice. Where there is no political freedom, privilege and injustice creep back."

But privilege and injustice exist equally well where there is no economic freedom, and it is completely inconsistent to claim, as Attlee does, that there can be any real political freedom in a society where economy is planned by the State, any more than in a society where it is controlled by capitalist monopolies.

In fact, there is only a difference of practice, not of principle, between the various social systems of America, Britain and Russia. All are based ultimately and fundamentally on coercion, and the amount of coercion they use is based on the needs of the ruling class. America has not a State-controlled economy, because private capitalism can still work there for the time being. Britain has as yet no full-scale NKVD because the government can rule without it by means of propaganda and deception. But America has its political pogroms, Britain has its interference with the freedom of workers to find their own employment, and if it were in the interests of the ruling class these institutions could easily be magnified into something resembling the Soviet tyranny. These three political systems in fact are all versions of the same State society, and social circumstances are steadily making them draw together in their internal forms, if not in their external interests.

If, as Attlee contends, it is possible to have political freedom with a State-planned economy, then the first thing he should do is to repeal all the laws and regulations which hamper the freedom of the people of this country. In fact, he could not do this if he wished, since the structure of a State economy depends on compulsion, the degree of which will be dictated by the amount of potential resistance among the people.

Inevitably Attlee's speech has been widely interpreted as anti-Russian. It is true that he criticises American capitalism, but very mildly. On the other hand, he tells us that "America stands for individual liberty . . . ", whereas in fact recent events have shown, through the political persecution of American minorities, that the governing class of the U.S.A. is only willing to recognise individual liberty where this suits its interests.

In the same way, Attlee condemns the Russian sponsoring of tyrannical régimes in Eastern Europe. But he does not say anything about the American support for reactionary governments in Greece and Turkey, which are just as prone to intense political persecutions as are the Communist régimes of Eastern Europe and the Balkans. American warships are sailing in Greek waters, American soldiers are in Turkey, to ensure the stability of governments which at no stretch of the imagination can be called democratic, except in the preverted sense used by the Russian puppet States.

In spite of all Attlee's ingenuity of argument, Britain, by its own attacks on individual liberty and participation in American imperialist ventures, shows itself of a similar nature to the régimes of Russia and America—the difference is only in degree, and different social circumstances can readily change that.

There is indeed a third way. But it lies only in opposition to any kind of State, for, where the State continues, the restriction of freedom at home and imperialist ventures abroad are inevitable.

January, 1948.

NEITHER EAST NOR WEST

WE HAVE received the following letter criticising the articles which appeared in *Freedom* on the 15th November:

"I am surprised and disgusted at the blatant and virulent anti-Russian war propaganda, published in your articles on 'Repression in Eastern Europe'.

Such propaganda makes it very difficult for those of us who are trying to save civilization from atomic destruction. One of your articles says that Russian domination in any country will bring poverty and famine and preparation for a new war. This is very unfair since the acute famine in some countries of Eastern Europe is due to the fact that a major world war has been fought over their territory, also due to the fact that their 'national independence' of pre-war years consisted of very reactionary governments, who kept these countries in a backward state.

Elsewhere you say: 'Russia does not care about the millions of dead in the war. It has enabled her to become the greatest power in the world, second to the U.S.A.' Have you forgotten that many of the dead were Russians and that the Russian people suffered quite as much, and more in the world war, as the countries of Eastern Europe? The fact is, of course, that Russian Imperialism treats the countries of Eastern Europe as colonial subjects, in exactly the same fashion that Great Britain treats her overseas territories. What about the colour bar in South Africa? The pestilential conditions in the West Indies? What about the brutal capitalism and the terrible racial discrimination that poisons American life and also the threatened enslavement of America to militarist and nationalist principles? There are very few articles in your paper, I notice, about those things, especially about conditions in the British Empire.

Capitalist principles are doing enough to drag America, ourselves and the whole world towards war, without your paper printing capitalist propaganda and making it easy for the war-mongers of the world.

Imperialists there are indeed in Russia, but we also have plenty nearer home. We can do nothing about Eastern Europe's trials, only the people of Eastern Europe and Russia can do that, but we can do something about the tension between the nations and about conditions in the British Empire and in the U.S.A.

I do not agree with any Imperialism whatever and I certainly don't think that Russia is any better than any other country, in fact, her foreign policy gets nearer to that of the Romanoffs every day. I, however, have no wish to see San Francisco, Sydney, Moscow, Edinburgh or any other great city of the world go the same way as Hiroshima did, and so will not make any effort to take sides in a conflict which is the direct result of the Vansittart-Ehrenburg policy which led to Potsdam.

Nationalist wars never produce any good thing. The next one may produce a crop of dictators if it does not destroy us all first."

Our correspondent would be absolutely right in denouncing us for war-mongering, if we attacked Russian imperialism while at the same time defending Britain and America. By taking a quotation out of its context she misrepresents our intention. The article from which she quotes, after stating that: "Russian domination is the end of every freedom; it brings poverty and famine, it is the prelude to another war", immediately goes on to say: "This conviction does not lead us to seek refuge in the arms of British or American Imperialism. We realise, on the contrary, that Russia's strength lies in the fact that her only opponents are as corrupted and ruthless as she is herself. As long as Socialist and other parties will fight Communism hiding behind America's skirts, they are bound to be defeated."

In other words, we denounce the very attitude which our correspondent accuses us of taking.

She further misquotes us when she makes us say: "Russia does not care about the millions of dead in the war"; we said in fact: "Zhdanov may have reasons to be satisfied by the results of the war . . ." By Zhdanov we meant the Rulers of Russia whom he represents on the Cominform. We are the last to forget the sufferings of the Russian people and that is why we charge the Russian Government with having sacrificed millions of Russian lives to their imperialist aspirations.

We would not waste space to point out to our reader that she has misread our articles if the misunderstanding did not arise from an attitude which is fairly widespread in Left-wing circles and which makes many people, who have no sympathy for Stalin's régime, extremely sensitive to any attack on that régime.

Their attitude is very similar to that of many socialists and pacifists who, in pre-war years, looked with disapproval upon violent denunciations of Hitler's régime because they saw in it a furthering of war. This fear of war led them to support non-intervention in Spain and the Munich pact.

We now have the appeasers of Russia. They are so hypnotised by the vision of atomic war that they are prepared to turn a blind eye on crimes committed under their very noses.

We wholly disagree with this attitude. We do not think that war can be avoided by a policy which entails the suppression of facts. We hold this view for ethical reasons, but also for practical ones. Ethical: because we do not believe in suppressing truth to suit a certain policy; this would be propaganda in the pejorative sense which our correspondent gives to that word. We are not interested in "propaganda". We denounced the Russian régime during the war at a time when everybody was praising Stalin, from Mr. Churchill downwards. If we were concerned in furthering "capitalist propaganda" we would not have chosen to say unpopular truths all these years.

We cannot alter our views about Russia simply because, for imperialist reasons, American and British spokesmen now denounce Russian totalitarianism. We know that their indignation is hypocritical and that they may become friendly to Russia again if it suits their interests. But for all that, are we to stifle our own indignation?

The practical reasons are equally important. We do not believe that a policy of appeasement towards Stalin will prevent war any more than the policy of appeasement towards Hitler stopped the last one. The only way to prevent wars is to abolish the causes of wars. Wars are inherent in totalitarian régimes, and therefore we denounce totalitarianism wherever we find it. We have denounced it in America, in India, in Greece and Palestine. We have always advocated complete independence for British colonies; we have demanded the abolition of the armed forces; we have fought for the defence of civil liberties with all the strength at our command.

Our correspondent challenges our statement that Russian domination will bring poverty and famine to Eastern Europe. We based our statement on two main observations: (a) that before the war, Russia experienced several famines due to forced collectivisations and bureaucratic blunders, and (b) that, though war is partly responsible for the critical situation in Eastern Europe, Russia's policy, of appropriating to herself industrial equipment and raw materials from the countries under her domination, prevents economic recovery. By isolating the Eastern countries from the rest of Europe she is further preventing the normal exchange of goods between East and West.

We also refuse to accept the statement that the trials which are now taking place in Europe should not concern us. It may be true that our protests will not change the course of events, but we must voice them nevertheless. Workers all over the world who rallied to the defence of Sacco and Vanzetti were not able to save them from the electric chair, yet who can say that their protests were useless?

We shall denounce political trials, whether they are held in Washington or in Warsaw. When a government puts a man in jail for his political opinions, we do not ask the nationality of that government. We are always on the side of the victim of State tyranny.

We hate war and have consistently fought against it and for that reason we fight State oppression wherever it occurs.

December, 1947.

INDEX